WHAT *is the* PURPOSE *of my*

BRAIN?

WHAT *is the* PURPOSE *of my* BRAIN?

Spiritual Healing and Salvation

DR. PAUL NUSSBAUM

TATE PUBLISHING
AND **ENTERPRISES**, LLC

Published by Tate Publishing & Enterprises, LLC
127 E. Trade Center Terrace | Mustang, Oklahoma 73064 USA
1.888.361.9473 | www.tatepublishing.com

Tate Publishing is committed to excellence in the publishing industry. The company reflects the philosophy established by the founders, based on Psalm 68:11,
"The Lord gave the word and great was the company of those who published it."

Book design copyright © 2016 by Tate Publishing, LLC. All rights reserved.
Cover design by Samson Lim
Interior design by Mary Jean Archival

Published in the United States of America

ISBN: 978-1-68319-704-1
1. Religion / Psychology of Religion
2. Religion / Spirituality
16.04.13

To the Holy Spirit
who fills us with love and forgiveness

Contents

Preface
The Pivots of Life

In 1994, I made a major pivot in my life when something spiritual stopped me and reminded me that I entered my profession because of my interest in health across the life span. Funny thing that happens to some of us who have completed postgraduate clinical training: the focus is all upon disease, and so the training produces relatively robotic thinkers. This is not a malicious set of events, but it is the truth, and it is why our medical approach has a very difficult time incorporating the real medicines that are most valued and needed by human beings. Having said that, I still believe we have the best health-care system in the world.

My first pivot was inspired by my discontent with my robotic focus on disease, and I was led to a rather radical shift in my career that focused on thinking, writing, and speaking about health and, more specifically, about brain health. Further, my audience moved from the academic community, where I spent much time with the general public, and—as I like to say—to "the mothers and fathers across the dinner tables." My seemingly driven passion for the human brain interfaced with my interest in health, and in 2002, I presented a major keynote at the American Society on Aging that bridged the animal research findings of how the environment can shape the rodent brain to the human brain. This was the formal start of my work in the area of brain health. The keynote led to my first book (Nussbaum 2003) on the topic of brain health and wellness and to my Brain Health Lifestyle® (see fig. 1) that I have taught to over one hundred thousand people of all backgrounds over the past twenty years and now fuels the energy in my brain health center (see www.brainhealthctr.com).

Figure 1. Dr. Nussbaum's Brain Health Lifestyle®.

The significance of my first pivot—to focus on health, to work primarily with the general public, and to work with all sectors of society to become enlightened to the miracle of the human brain and how each of us can shape our brains for health across the life span—was indeed life changing. I have had the enormous blessing of speaking to and meeting so many people in the United States, Canada, and Europe. The inspiring stories I have heard can fill a separate book, and they have certainly filled me with enormous respect and admiration for the human spirit. I also realized that when I speak, I am being guided by a higher power and a Spirit that has enabled me to connect with so many in ways that are deeply personal. Now I believe I am once again being led by a Higher Spirit to make a second, perhaps even greater, pivot that revolves around a basic question: *What is the purpose of my brain?*

This book explores an overarching issue that supersedes matters of anatomy, behavior, disease, and the brilliant complexity of the brain. By asking about the purpose of my brain, I move beyond the traditional topics of anatomy and behavior to questions dealing with our very existence, our connection to the universe, and why the brain might be the conduit for both. This is my pivot since I am now thinking about grand issues of existence that stretch beyond neurons and neurochemicals and brain health. I do believe the human brain is the single greatest system ever designed, and I have spent many hours in front of thousands expressing this belief.

However, now my own brain and the spiritual energy of my brain is asking a basic question: If I believe the brain is such a miracle, then might it have a grand purpose?

I want to know why it was designed. I do not believe humans, our brains, or our universe is random. I have now moved into a spiritual realm—some might say too late—but nonetheless, this is where my journey has carried me. I believe I was placed on a path that began at least twenty years ago to teach others about the miracle of their brain and to bring hope to their lives. Now I will try to express my thoughts about the human brain from a spiritual perspective and to bring hope to those who read my words. Once again, I will tell you that the words come to me from a spiritual presence I am blessed to experience, and this book reflects a personal journey I believe I am supposed to take and share.

After nearly thirty years of professional life and over fifty in total, I now realize how little I know; and in my third quarter of life, I find myself asking more questions and not finding the answers from my clinical or academic bodies of knowledge. I know there are realities of life, of human behavior, human spirit, and the universe that we simply cannot explain. I am attempting, therefore, to unite my relatively little knowledge of Christian scripture, the universe, and the human brain into a potentially cohesive story without any pretense of a conclusion.

I am a follower of Jesus Christ with infinite faith in him and his teachings. Regardless of what one thinks of Jesus, there is little doubt, even from staunch atheists, that his life was about love, forgiveness, and caring. I believe it is he who imparted his Holy Spirit that guided my first pivot. It is he who, through his Spirit, helps me to bring hope to others when I speak about the miracle of the brain and how we can shape it for health no matter our age. I now believe it is Jesus who again is guiding me with his Spirit to make this second, and perhaps even more significant, pivot in my life and career. For that, I am humble and grateful.

The human brain is indeed the single most magnificent miracle ever designed, and it sits directly between our ears. It serves as the origin of our every thought, emotion, and behavior; and it both builds and carries our *life story*, perhaps the *most precious* gift we have. Our brain connects us to ourselves, providing us a unique identity, and enables us to relate to others. Why is it important that we have an identity? Our brain also permits our processing of the universe around us that we view as distinct yet connected to us. Our ability to know we are unique, distinct from others and other things, distinct from the universe and indeed from God, and yet capable of communing with each is a foundationally powerful capacity of the human brain. This and the other incredibly complex abilities of our brain lead me to ask, Who or what designed the brain, and why is it important that we connect to ourselves, others, and to the universe?

Imagine, I have been speaking to thousands of people about what I call the single greatest miracle ever designed, and only now am I stopped and called to ponder the critical point that if I truly believe the brain is a miracle and that it was designed for us with all of its presumed complexity, what then does this necessitate? For me, it requires that I ask and attempt to answer the question I have raised for this book about the purpose of having a brain and who or what designed it? This book is my attempt to begin this exploration of a purpose for my brain by turning to neuropsychology, spirituality, the fundamental philosophical interface of the two, and their basic practicality.

Perhaps God gave us our brain for a consciousness, for a conduit or medium to enable his intent for us to witness and divorce self, relate to others, and commune with our universe near and beyond. Perhaps God gave us our brain to communicate with him and to understand his intent for us, including an appreciation of right from wrong and heaven from hell. From our brain, we have the ability to understand and to believe in the Holy Spirit, which is expressed through our brain in the form of what I call *neural energy*. It is from this energy and Spirit that we can impact and connect with our internal being, others around us, and even the vast universe and God. As such, the human brain is an energy source capable of connecting with other energy sources, and our spiritual being is indeed one form of energy. Perhaps it is the brain that expresses God's Holy Spirit beyond the life of our body and keeps us connected with him and our universe eternally (beyond the flesh).

These ideas provide hope and a sense of safety and protection within a grand scheme of love that is beyond our current understanding. It enables us to close our eyes and whisper, "It is okay, and I am okay." Such a statement and feeling brings peace and balance to our brain that is so often fraught with anxiety and big worry about small things. Such ideas also have the ability to take us beyond the tangible and finite existence here on Earth. Anxiety and fear cease to exist when we believe and have faith that our existence has a grander purpose and place than earthbound offerings.

I am asserting that the human brain is far too complicated to be random, that we know very little about the brain's capacity, and that the brain is an energy source that we will one day tap and change civilization with for the better. There can only be one author for such a miracle, and that is God; and the same can be said for the universe, a system not unlike the human brain. It is of interest that scripture tells us that God made us in his image. This might offer a clue as to the purpose of my brain, and that purpose may indeed be to *commune with God*.

My intent with this book is to share my thoughts on these matters and to take another small step in my spiritual journey with my second pivot, doing the work I am called to do. I hope everyone who reads this book finds comfort, hope, and a renewed sense of faith and love that can help each connect more deeply with the spiritual energy and power that lies within you. It is from our Spiritual energy, granted to us by

God and working within our brain, that real healing, wellness, and that eternal connection to God and the universe can occur. It is from this internal Spirit that we can *love others as we ourselves wish to be loved.* As I write this book, I am keenly aware of the terror, trauma, horror, and evil that pervades our world. I can think of no better time than now to turn to the prescription for neurospiritual healing outlined in this book.

This book is not a scientific manuscript or a religious doctrine. It is a personal and humble attempt to integrate thirty years of clinical science, observing human behavior, practicing my Christian faith, offering clinical care, listening, and remaining in awe of the *human spirit*, the *grand universe*, and my need to bridge the two. I ask questions, and I do my best to answer, understanding that sometimes there is no answer. I am asking another question with this book that takes me, and anyone reading it, to the very essence of our existence from the perspective of our brain. For me, it is a highly cathartic exercise and expression of my faith that what I believe is real and how these ideas have the ability to empower all to heal within, to experience balance and peace, to know we are part of a greater story, to express our positive influence on others with love, particularly those in need, and to know that our body is simply a time-limited and earthbound structure that carries our eternally connected Spirit.

I do hope that my words bring you some peace, love, and hope, particularly if you read this book with a sense of loss and despair. To the most unfortunate and those tormented with fear, anxiety, hatred, hunger, isolation, grief, pain, and illness, I wish to share my own Spirit and energy with you so that you may feel the love and peace through these words as part of our connected neural energy. For those who remain closed to this message and perhaps to the healing and loving spirit within you, I extend an extra prayer. So many are searching for their inner balance and spiritual connection in products, foods, and other forms of man-made and earthbound healing. I will tell you that the greatest source of healing, of happiness, of peace, and of love lies within you, and it was given you prior to your entry into this world. This book encourages all to be open to this eternal source of spiritual energy, which originates from our three-pound miracle gift that sits between your own ears. Your search is over!

SECTION 1

Exploring the Purpose

1

Introduction

The wind blows where it wishes and you hear
the sound of it, but cannot tell where it goes.
So is everyone who is born of the spirit.

—John 3:8

At three-thirty in the morning, my wife woke me to walk outside on the deck of our vacation rental to gaze at the stars above. Everyone knows the night sky is filled with lights, but sometimes one's attention is commanded, and a quiet sense of awe arrives, causing stillness. This was the case for me that early morning in the summer of 2015. My eyes saw thousands of stars, the Milky Way galaxy, and at least ten shooting stars. From the distance, I could hear the rhythmic waves of the Atlantic Ocean that broke against an otherwise quiet stillness. At these moments, I get a distinct sense that there exist powers, forces, energies that are real and with us, but far greater than our ability to appreciate or comprehend. My brain began to raise questions about myself, human existence, the Earth, the universe, God, whether we are all connected, and if everything is random. All good stuff but beyond our ability to answer, so we are left to speculate, to turn to science and to strong opinions, none of which provides the answers. This leaves questions, and many may simply sleep well knowing those answers are out of reach and perhaps part of God's plan. I tend to be one who obsesses on these questions and to try and do my best to provide reasonable ideas that make some sense at least for me.

The human brain, like the thousands of stars I saw in the early morning sky in 2015, also inspires awe, stillness, and respect. The brain is also a system, like the universe, that we do not understand, that medicine and science do not have answers for, and yet we all realize how powerful this three-pound mass of cells and fat is. It seems to me there may be a connection between the vast, complicated, not-yet-understood universe that projects to us via thousands of stars each night, making us feel small, and the infinite power of our own electrical and chemical energy source, our not-yet-understood human brain, that serves as the origin of our every thought, emotion, and behavior. It is, after all, our brains that processes and interacts with the universe; and it is my brain that permits me to speculate about such things, right or wrong. I began to wonder, Is there something more about the human brain and the universe, something not yet understood but worth considering?

There are indeed vast sources of energy, grand powers that surround us every day and are with us at all times. The human brain is also the single greatest, most magnificent miracle ever designed in my opinion, and it sits right between our ears and is with us each and every day. Might these two distinct energy sources of perhaps infinite power be connected? And if they were not simply a random or chance creation, might there be an even grander author of the two who wants to inspire communion between both, offering a window to the purpose of our brains?

This book begins and ends with a basic question, *What is the purpose of the human brain?* Is the brain primarily an incredibly complex system that enables our cognition, emotion, behavior, and motor ability to manifest each day while we are alive? Does the brain really have a finite existence like the human body, functioning only about eighty years on the planet Earth? There is nothing to be ashamed about if this is the only purpose of our brain and if we really only have a relatively brief period of time to perform such functions. Somehow I cannot believe that such a magnificent system as the human brain is without a greater purpose and that it is limited by time and age. I do believe there is a far greater purpose to the brain. I believe the brain has the ability to shape and heal our internal organism; to connect with energies, forces, and powers outside of us; and to keep us connected and in communion with the grand universe even beyond the demise of our body, with the structure that carries our energy, our Spirit. One day, I believe we will better understand this and be able to apply the power of our brain, and civilization will be changed for the better. We are not advanced enough yet to understand the what, how, or why of the ideas I am discussing, but that will change one day.

Our brains contain an energy source I refer to as *neural energy*, which we can learn to use not only for personal healing but to connect with other energies and powers around us. I will turn to scripture as a means of suggesting where such energy and power might be derived and how the human brain may be a conduit granted us in order to commune with natural energies that surround us each day and night and perhaps even enable our spirit to remain connected with the universal powers forever.

Flow of the Book

I am a neuropsychologist by training, and my expertise lies in the areas of neuroanatomy and behavior and the relationship between the two. This book deviates from my areas of expertise, and it is important for me to say and for you to know that I am not an expert in energy, physics, astronomy, religion, or the Bible. I know human behavior, the human brain, and I am not afraid to ask questions. I also know that science and medicine do not have answers to what I am writing about in this book.

The good news is that there is a growing interface between the sciences and religion or spiritual realms of life, and that is a positive thing since the human being is a spiritual being and such matters have always affected health and balance in the lives of humans.

On a purely selfish note, I want to put into writing my awe about the many things in nature that make us wide-eyed, my passion about the human brain as the single most complicated miracle ever designed, and a strong sense that the two are not distinct. Indeed, I want to try and express my belief that a grand author has brought the two powers and sources of energy together as a means of magnificent and eternal communion. I believe scripture is therefore necessary for guidance to explore the tie that binds the brain to the majesty of the universe and the role God might have in this.

This book will provide a scripture reading with a citation that introduces each chapter and is meant to provoke meditation on the scripture and how it might have meaning for the content of the chapter and the primary question of the book, What is the purpose of my brain? The book opens with a discussion and overview of what I refer to as *neural energies* and how such energies are innate to the brain and set the foundation for shaping our brains and bodies, connecting it with others and communing with forces outside of our beings perhaps forever (an internal-external conduit). I attempt to connect neural energies to our God-given spiritual being that enables the connections from internal to external.

The book then provides a series of short chapters that focus on the importance of being open to those external and surrounding energies provided by nature, the universe, and ultimately, God. These chapters will provide examples of real-life events that illustrate the potentially deeper meanings of particular behaviors, words, and experiences in nature that we tend to remain closed to. External forces may be interacting and communicating with us, but we will not understand or appreciate this if we are closed. From there, the book begins to suggest a new way of looking at the brain that goes beyond an anatomical or behavioral approach to one that explores what the brain desires: balance and a natural rhythm. The idea of God having a purpose for our brain is reinforced. This is naturally followed by a chapter in which I turn to the teachings of Christ in the hopes of generating some guidance to the primary question posed by this book.

From these early chapters, the remainder of the book seeks to explore how our spiritual being, our neural energies, can be applied in our own journey toward balance and health, as well as a robust communion with energies that exist beyond the human realm. I titled the closing section of the book "Our Neurospirtual Path," which provides short chapters on specific "fruits of the spirit." We call these emotions and feeling states expressed and experienced by our Spirit that can bring personal healing and balance, a path to unity with others, and even communion with our universe and God.

Our spiritual energy may have been granted us by a Higher Being who or that is always near and I believe is connected with us, but we need to be open. It is this innate Spirit and energy that resides within us, that connects us to others, to the universe, and it likely remains connected forever. The journey interestingly begins internally, with a focus of where each of us is regarding our beliefs and openness to such energy and Spirit. Our lives provide us so many examples of such energy and spiritual interplay, yet we are not typically mindful of such activity, and we are quick to simply call it odd or a miracle. This book seeks to probe deeper; and since our brain is the epicenter of our being, including our spiritual being, and serves as the conduit to energies and forces external to us, the question remains, What is the purpose of my brain? (For purposes of this text, I will use terms *energy*, *forces*, *powers*, and *spirit* interchangeably. When *Spirit* is capitalized, it refers to a godly presence.)

Let us begin.

2

Neural Energy

For what man knows the things of a man except the
spirit of the man which is in him? Even so no one
knows the things of God except the Spirit of God.
Now, we have received not the spirit of the world, but
the Spirit who is from God; that we might know the
things that have been freely given to us by God.

—Corinthians 3:11–12

What in the world is neural energy? *Neural* is defined as "nerve or having to do with the nervous system." I created the term to refer to the dynamic source of energy created and used by the human brain. I use the term to reinforce a basic premise: *the human brain is an energy source, an electrical and chemical energy source.* As with any energy source, there is a dynamic nature to it; and we know the human brain serves as the epicenter for our every thought, emotion, and movement. It is the grandest of all complicated systems and what I refer to as the single greatest, most magnificent miracle ever designed in the history of this or any universe. The energy from the brain does indeed affect and influence our inner workings and internal homeostasis. We are the only living organism on the planet that can make ourselves miserable or happy from a thought. Indeed, as I teach my audiences across the planet, the message or thought you place in your brain carries the blueprint for the rest of your body. This idea has tremendous implications for the question of this book and deserves the critical attention of all.

Part of the purpose of this book is to think about the significant role our brains have over our health and well-being. The energy produced and expressed by the brain should have an influence over the systems of our body. This is the brain's influence over our internal being. Another equally important purpose of this book is to review an idea that the human brain, through neural energies can and does connect with and influence energy in our external world as well. In essence, the human brain serves as the *energy* or *spiritual conduit* to shape and affect our internal organism and to connect us with energy and powers that exist outside and distinct from the brain. This is the way we can affect others around us and even connect with spirits and powers of nature that are not human. A more compelling question emerges from this foundational belief in neural energy: Does our brain have a greater purpose, and might it be within our skulls as part of this greater purpose?

I have worked for nearly twenty-five years with persons suffering from neurological, neurodegenerative, and neuropsychiatric disorders. I have spent even more time studying neuroanatomy, behavior, and neuropsychology in general. The traditional approach of discussing parts of the brain and the behaviors that relate to them, the behaviors and cognitive skills that change or decline with age, and the latest neurodiagnostic formulations to provide earlier detection to diseases remain important. However, I am now most interested in asking different questions about the human brain. I believe there are inherent powers and abilities of the human brain yet undefined or undiscovered. Perhaps we are too primitive a species to understand that a more enhanced brilliance exists within our brain, or maybe we are conceptually closed off from such an exploration or acceptance of what was taught us many years ago. Might this energy source of the brain I refer to as neural energy be the spiritual gift provided us by God as expressed in Corinthians above?

My belief is that all the answers to our questions as humans lie within the folds and flaps of our *cortex*; that neural energy has the ability to heal within, to connect with other brains in new ways, to connect forever with powers and energy sources external to us; and I believe that if we can learn how to tap our neural energy and how to be open to natural energies and powers that surround us, we will advance our civilization in ways not yet realized. These are the interesting and compelling thoughts and questions that motivated me to write a book, if for no other reason than to put on paper what I have been observing, considering, and dreaming about for many years.

So take a deep breath and get prepared to be open to think deeply about yourself, about people and forces around you, and about our position within the grand universe. Common daily behaviors and interactions might have more meaning than we appreciate, but we need to be open to such meaning. Conversations and thoughts might actually provide a prelude of what is to occur or is occurring at the same time as the actual thought. Our *will* is more than a word, and indeed, our thoughts and words do have significant power over our health and well-being, perhaps even the health of others. Sometimes such will and belief cure terminal conditions, and we do not know how because we are not open to the answers. Is there a grander force or power that guides us and is present with us? Is the brain the conduit for connecting with this force that I refer to as God? What is the binding connection of human to human and human to the external energies, including God or a higher being? I believe it is the *brain* and the *neural energy* born from the brain. I believe further that God created the brain so that we might have the ability to connect and be affected by such higher forces.

These issues are not standard neuropsychology 101, and I purposely want to direct our time and attention within the pages of this book to a healthy introspection and consideration of these and other similar questions. In so doing, we learn about ourselves and one another. We consider our place in a vast universe, and we ponder why and how. We can take some solace in knowing that as simple as our species might be, we do carry with us a three-pound miracle more capable than anything we know with untapped neural energy. Yet what is the purpose of this miracle, and why do we have such power?

3

Pennies in My Path and Our Need to Be Open

> While we do not look at the things which are
> seen, but at the things, which are not seen. For
> the things that are seen are temporary but the
> things which are not seen are eternal.
>
> —Corinthians 4:18

Exercise 1: Open versus Closed

I would like you to stand tall in a relaxed position. Take a deep breath. Now open your arms to the side of your body with your palms facing up and be as open and wide as you can be. Pretend you are going to hug all your favorite people in life and open those arms so everyone can be included.

Close your eyes and experience what this feels like. What are the feelings, sensations, and thoughts associated with this position? Before you open your eyes, I want you to *smile* (recall a wonderful or funny moment) and experience how your body reacts to the smile.

Now relax again, and this time, I want you to take both arms and hug yourself tightly, wrapping both arms around yourself without hurting yourself. If you want, bend over a bit and become closed off. Hold this position for fifteen seconds and pay close attention to how you feel and what emotions and thoughts you might experience in this position.

Now relax and again, stand tall, and open your arms real wide with palms facing upward to the sky as you stretch them out to your side. *Smile* (recall a wonderful or funny moment). What are the feelings you experience? Are you able to distinguish the difference between a body position that permits openness and one that is closed off?

Are you open or closed in your own life?

(To all my amateur and professional photographer friends, the brain knows the difference between a *cortical smile* and *subcortical smile*. The best smile is the subcortical smile as it is spontaneous and natural. It is also robust, filled with joy and bliss. The cortical smile is staged, unnatural, and artificial. We all want to work on our subcortical smiles, so recall moments that bring you great laughter, and you will smile subcortically. If you are asked to smile, the cortex will respond, but it will be artificial.)

Powers External to Us Influence Us

I am the product of a highly structured clinical and scientific training that lasted eleven years post-high school and resulted in my great fortune of being taught by intelligent and creative people. I have never deviated from the empirical approach to observation and measurement, and I continue to have a deep appreciation for the scientific method. Twenty-five plus years of working in the clinical and scientific arena has also taught me that there are realities that cannot be explained by empiricism or any scientific method. Sometimes we refer to such occurrences as *odd*, an *outlier*, or *miraculous*. Things happen every day that we cannot explain, and that is a fact. This is most interesting, particularly for someone like me who is fascinated by human behavior and what shapes our behavior across the life span.

I often wonder what and where the forces are that guide the universe, create energies between people, and also impact our own inner functioning. Is there a rationale for all that occurs, or do things happen simply by chance? Perhaps both are true; but if there is an energy, force, or power that exists extrinsic yet related to us, it would be important to know more about it so we could develop and utilize it. Fun questions to ponder on a warm evening after a hard day of work!

For me, I have experienced too much and seen too much to not believe that such a power exists, and I further believe that such power or energy does influence our organism to believe or think certain things, to make particular decisions, to act or move in a particular manner, and to feel a certain way, good or bad. That does not mean we do not have free will, but here again, where does the free will come from? To me, the power may lie extrinsic to us, but I believe we have the ability to interact with this power and to enable it to influence our lives. Perhaps even more importantly, we then have the ability to influence other lives! I am a Christian and believe in God as such an extrinsic yet interrelated power that guides and shapes our being. For others, forces of nature and energies exist that might not be attributed to God or a higher being. The important point to consider is whether or not you are open to such an energy force or power that you can interact with, be shaped by, and utilize in your daily life.

My career over the past twenty years has involved a significant amount of travel inside and outside the United States as I carry a passionate message on brain health to all receptive brains I can find. I have had the great pleasure of meeting so many interesting people with diverse backgrounds who have a story to share. It is from these interactions that I have developed a true and inspiring sense of the *human spirit* (an interesting term that I do not think we fully consider or understand) and all that it can accomplish. We humans often achieve greater accomplishments and survive more supposed malignant diseases than what is predicted by the informed medical, scientific, or empirical fields.

I often am curious how the human spirit overrides such hard-and-fast rules, probabilities, or assumptions. My sense is that the human spirit is part of the energy and force I have been discussing so far. When it is tapped in a consistent way, the human spirit may indeed have the ability to survive, overcome, and adapt to realities that are typically terminal or catastrophic. Perhaps this reflects the power of faith, belief, and surrender of self to forces and energy that can heal and triumph. It represents openness to the miracles of our day. Perhaps it is the alignment of our own internal neural energy with powers extrinsic to us that facilitate success and positive outcomes.

We may understand this inner power one day, and that will be a good and revolutionary thing because it appears to provide our species with an intrinsic healing power and an ability to shape outcomes around us. Society today, at least in the United States, seems to be moving away from God and the formalized practice of religion. This is unfortunate as it is not only foundational to our nation and development as a species (regardless of particular practice or belief), but research continues to build on the relationship between formalized religious practice and health (Koenig 1999; Newberg and Waldman 2010). Words such as *faith*, *belief*, *attitude*, and *will* are often used to describe forms of energy or spirit in humans. These are active forces, and while we tend not to think about their effects, I often talk about my belief that such words actually activate the brain in specific ways to then activate the body and perhaps the survival and healing mechanism.

Certainly, this is one of the primary foundations of the mind-body and psychoneuroimmunology approach popular to many. It also fuels my belief in the power of neural energy over the structure and function of our being. Even at the basic level in controlled studies, we still do not understand fully the idea of placebo and why nearly 25 percent of a study sample demonstrates outcomes typically only explained by "treatment" interventions. It might be a good thing to better understand what is occurring with placebo and whether there is some force, energy, or power that can influence outcomes. Perhaps mere suggestion or deep belief are real and have physical, psychological, and spiritual influences on our being. Survival is a natural state, and we behave consciously in ways that support our desire to survive. Given the importance of survival, it is hard for me to believe we did not come equipped with powers that influence favorably our ability to survive. One thing is for sure: the placebo effect is not going away, and I rather assume that its effect will only grow as our culture learns more about mindfulness and matters of neural energy.

For me, the power I am describing involves the brain; and perhaps the brain serves as the generator, channel, or port for the creation, flow, and targeting of such power derived from outside our brain. Perhaps the brain is all three, I do not know. The brain has the complexity to generate such a force, to recognize and interact with forces external to us, and the ability to integrate the internal and external forces or energy in targeted and purposeful ways. Given the shear and unknowable power of the human brain, at least at this time in our evolution, I believe it to be the epicenter of such phenomena. Our ability to understand and to tap this power that lies between our ears will one day revolutionize and forward society and our species forever. In my opinion, the human brain is an incredibly untapped source of energy, and as we evolve, our ability to tap this energy source will emerge.

Being Open to Powers in My Own Life

In my travels over the years, I've observed something that, at first, seemed a bit trivial and random. Later, I began to pay closer attention as the phenomena continued to happen with some regularity. Naturally, I began to wonder whether this was something more than a simple random event or coincidence. Regardless of where I was or what the circumstances were, I'd notice a penny on the ground in front of me. Sometimes, the penny appeared old and worn, as though it was punished by the elements of nature. Sometimes it was shiny and glimmering with that distinctive copper glow of a new coin. Regardless, it was there in my path, and I'd feel a need to act, to pick it up. I had been taught as a child that when you find a penny, good luck would come your way. Naturally, I wanted to grab the penny and hope for my good fortune, but I never considered anything more about this. Today I wonder about that lesson taught to me and question who or what brings me the luck? I now refer to this regular experience in my life as *pennies in my path.*

I began to pay closer attention as more and more pennies showed up in my path. My belief that there is a force, energy, and a spiritual power placing these pennies before me in my path as I move in life emerged slowly. I continue to pick them up, believing also that some good luck will come my way even though I am not completely sure who or what brings me such luck. I recall a relatively recent and pronounced example of pennies in my path. I was to deliver a keynote address on brain health to a large audience on Hilton Head Island in early 2015. After a lovely introduction, I made my way to the microphone that was attached to a cord. Just prior to my saying thank-you for the kind words, my eyes scanned the ground in front of me to make sure I did not trip. What did I see but a shiny, new penny! I felt a sense of warmth come over my brain and body as this was like home to me, and I chuckled a bit out loud into the microphone. I then informed the audience about what happened and what it meant to me.

If pennies are being placed in my path by an external power, what is the power, and why would this be happening? For me, the first question is easily answered by my belief in God. This answer may be different for others since so many find pennies on the ground and may simply chalk it up to randomness. I believe the second question is also easily answered in that I believe I am being guided to do what I do in life, and that is the essence of how a penny can have meaning if we are open.

I have spent the past twenty years teaching audiences of all ages about the miracle of the brain that sits between our ears and how we have the ability to shape our brains for health using a proactive and lifelong lifestyle (see Brain Health Lifestyle® at www.brainhealthctr.com). The impact of this work has been humbling to me and much more powerful than I can imagine. Many persons have shared significant emotion in their reaction to my message, and they explain the impact the words have on their lives. These interactions from strangers solidify my belief that I am doing what I am supposed to do, that an external and spiritual force is with me to express my message so that it has the positive impact it does. The pennies remind me to continue on this path, much like a row of lights guide a plane to the runway in the dark of night.

The message I share about the brain to all age-groups is not only educational but also empowering and, at times for some, life changing. My role as the communicator is being guided by an external force and has influenced my own inner ability to share the message that, in turn, affects favorably thousands of others. I feel quite blessed to have this opportunity and realize that the time I might be provided to deliver such a message to others is limited. The power of the word, belief, spirit, attitude, connection, touch, and so much more is the power we do not yet understand, but it is real. I have been led by it, and I have seen its powerful effect on others. Here again is a real-life experience that illustrates the impact of neural energies to empower and fuel my inner health and to shape the lives of so many in my surroundings. This is the internal-external connection I described earlier, the alignment and synergy of our spirit and energy with that outside us.

The only reason I noticed pennies in my path and the meaning it has for me in my life is that I learned to be open to the spiritual forces and energies that surround us. I have become quite humble in my life, realizing how little relevance and power I have. However, with humility comes a divorce from self and the ability to align with and to commune with others and the forces of nature where the power to triumph comes. My ability to communicate about complicated ideas to all age-groups is not my talent. It is a gift given me for a short period of time and one that I am being directed to deliver by a higher being as it is my role to help others through my words.

I realized this sometime ago and became quite mindful of how fortunate, even blessed, I am to have this opportunity. The pennies in my path bring me comfort and peace as I stated above because I know that God is leading me and that I am on the right path. From humility and a divorce of self, I became open to this medium of energy and spirit that is there for all of us. We just need to be open, and neural energy will emerge.

4

Being Open and Connected

I do believe we have a unique power and ability to connect with our inner workings and with energies outside our body. I think such connection and interaction of self to other occurs all the time, yet most are not even aware. In my humble opinion, we need to be open and to master the ability to be open to what occurs around us and how this activity might be attempting to connect with us. The small signs that others, nature, or events communicate to us are real and have meaning. Perhaps a conversation we have with someone contains critical words that trigger or serve as a prelude to future events. Maybe our observation of nature and what is shown us carries a meaning or a communication we can grasp and react to. The only way we can connect is to be open to such realities and to let ourselves be exposed to them with all their meaning.

In no uncertain terms, we need to be more conscious or mindful of our presence, our environment, and the interactions between the two. We tend to operate on a highly routinized and subconscious level with much of our behavior and perception. This can lead to us being closed off from others and from what nature and events are trying to teach us. We may be too busy on tasks or small details that we are missing bigger, grander opportunities to be drawn or guided and to shape or be shaped. Energies are all around us, and our brains have the wonderful ability to connect and process, to bring more meaning, and to enter a reality that goes beyond the tangible of here and now. It is time to be open and vigilant to the energy around us and to the signs being communicated to us.

Recall our exercise above when you opened your arms, closed your eyes, and smiled. Recall how you felt and how different that feeling was compared to when you hugged yourself and became closed off. This is a great exercise for you each morning and also during the day to generate openness and to be reminded about the miracles that can occur by being open. The following are personal examples in my own life of how the energy of events around us can carry a deeper meaning than we might otherwise think. The critical message is that by being open to such energy surrounding us, we have a chance to connect and to be informed, guided, and comforted in ways not possible if we remain closed.

Walk on the Beach

The final morning of our family vacation 2015 was spent walking along the beach with my wife. It was around 5:30 a.m., and the sun was beginning to rise just beyond the horizon. We had gotten word a day or two earlier that one of our family members who lived in the West was hospitalized and being cared for by professionals and a daughter. I was rather open that morning as I typically am when walking the beach so early and experiencing a sunrise over the Atlantic Ocean (see Appendix 2). I was accustomed to seeing dolphins, fish, and even stingray (see Appendix 2) in the shallow waters. Nature is always abundant, and the same was true on this particular morning.

One thing that was peculiar that morning was the rather extreme volume of fish jumping out of the water. This was so striking that I stopped my walk and became fixated on what nature was showing me as the sound of the fish jumping was distinct and rather powerful. It was even more compelling since, the night before, I attended a local church service and heard about the scripture where God provided bushels of fish for the masses of people who were hungry. My openness to what nature was providing me that morning in the context of what I learned from scripture the night before was not coincidental. I paused with some mixed emotion since, on the one hand, I knew I was connected with nature and a higher being providing me a message. This part of the experience is always wonderful and supernatural. However, I also knew rather quickly what the message was. My family member had passed away, and I was being told that he was okay, that Jesus had him, and that he was no longer in pain. When I got back to the home, I learned a couple of hours later that, around the time I saw the fish jumping by the hundreds in the Atlantic Ocean, my family member passed away. I felt blessed to have been open enough to experience this universal transition, especially through a most natural energy medium—not with a phone call, text, or e-mail.

Internal Spiritual Message

The night before I made my final walk on the beach and saw the hundreds of fish jumping, I attended a church service and then went with some family to a wonderful buffet. As noted above, we had a family member who was ill, and members of our family were headed home, leaving the rest of us at the beach. One of our family members who headed home was the spouse of the person who was ill and was naturally concerned with her loved one's condition. I was sitting in the car shortly after the mass, and I felt a presence or some type of information being communicated to me, which I processed and acted upon. I had a strong sense that my family member was going to die within twenty-four hours, and I immediately communicated to his spouse that she get to his side immediately after landing from the trip home.

As it turned out, I was correct, unfortunately, and our family member passed away that morning about the time I was observing the fish jumping with joy. We sometimes refer to this as a *gut sense* or a premonition. As many of us have such experiences, it is fair to consider this as a real yet unexplained phenomenon. I tend to think it is quite natural, quite frequent, and a communion of the external to our own internal energy or spirit. By being open, the connection is made possible, and an entire new reality becomes available to us.

My Friend's Fall

I live in a family-planned community where there is plenty of life in the form of young children playing, dogs running, and nature in abundance. My neighbors are wonderful people who are well educated and caring. My wife and I enjoy daily walks, and on one particular day, we met with our neighbors who were a pleasant married couple. I was struck by the fact they were walking too because they were avid runners, and I had such admiration for their ability to run with dedicated passion. As a result, they were also fit and trim and quite happy. I even joked with them that they should have been running and not simply walking like my wife and me!

Our conversation then turned to the fact that my wife and I noticed they were having some painting done on their home, and there was a tall ladder leaning against the side of their home. I offered a joke in which I told my neighbor-friend not to get on that ladder. We laughed and went our way, enjoying the sunny day.

Several days later, my wife and I learned the horrible news that an ambulance was in front of one of our neighbors' homes. We did not know about this, and upon further questioning, we learned that an ambulance had arrived urgently in front our neighbor's home (the same neighbors we met on our walk several days earlier) and that a man was taken to the hospital. We learned our neighbor had indeed climbed the ladder and fell directly onto his cement driveway, suffering a rather serious head injury.

Naturally, this sent immediate shock waves through my body as I realized the words I communicated to him and his wife days ago; and those words spoken with what I thought was within the context of a simple conversation had instead represented a premonition, a type of futuristic knowledge that none of us were open to. On the other hand, maybe I was open to it and offered my connection to it in a form of a joke. Perhaps I could have offered my openness and apparent connection to the future event with a more assertive and serious tone. I am happy to say that our friend and neighbor healed well and is back to running and being the model of fitness for our community.

These examples are real and a very small sample of how activity from nature, teachings from others, and conversations with friends represent energy that carries meaning, wanting to connect and guide us if we are open to it. Indeed, these are just three examples from my own life that occurred in a very narrow time frame, in just one year. Imagine all the similar experiences that can be shared by everyone reading this book across their entire life span. Imagine even further how much more we could or would have known or learned from our experiences if we had been open. Similarly, how much can we learn today and tomorrow by being open to what is being communicated to us by others or outside forces? How much can we learn by being open to what we are actually communicating to others with our communication, thoughts, and behavior? What is nature communicating to us? Can we accept that we are a part of a greater system built by God to live and interact in dynamic harmony?

Our brains represent the liaison, the channel, for such a connection and dynamic interaction. Further, I believe we are at a primitive stage of understanding these concepts and that there is much to develop and mature in as we advance as a species. I am convinced, however, that our brains have tremendous untapped potential and capacity that will permit us one day to not only better understand our ability to connect with others and with the energy and forces external to us but to actually engage in such communion.

This then offers a grander purpose to our brains and a possible path for our connection to the universe that is not only present during our time on Earth but beyond. Perhaps the fuel of such energy is our spiritual being as taught to us long ago. By being open, we can begin to develop the spiritual side of our own being and begin the process of connecting with others and with nature around us. Neural energy is with us to do such work and perhaps represents our human manifestation of the Spirit, but we need to be open.

5

A Different View of My Brain

The single greatest, most magnificent miracle ever designed

In one passage of the Bible (Genesis 1:27), it reads, "God created man in his own image." This is an interesting and telling statement as it infers that we humans are a reflection or model of God. For me, as well as others (Black and Mann 2009), *the* most salient example of this representation can be found in the complexity of the human brain. The truth of the matter is that we presently do not even understand what the brain can do as this level of insight is beyond our comprehension at this time. We can imagine, however—and it is my belief—that the brain will one day be able to fix the maladies of the human body and be able to communicate with other brains in a spiritual or energy medium, not simply by opening the mouth and speaking as we do today (neural energy).

Consider a recent study (Clark et al. 2014) that demonstrated muscle development in an injured or immobile limb simply from a person's thought of exercise (cortex-to-muscle activation). Case studies have also demonstrated how paralyzed individuals can move a cursor purely from thought (an electrical action) across a computer screen as a means of communicating. The cursor was moved on top of a letter one at a time so that a word was produced, permitting communication. Here again, we can appreciate the power of neural energies to affect the body within and to establish a connection without.

Perhaps even more striking, and approximating my ideas of neural energy, is the study of telepathy. A recent case was discussed in the media of a five-year-old savant with high-functioning autism who displays signs of being telepathic and is already learning seven languages. This child, who lives in the United States, was filmed being able to recite numbers written in secret, a behavior that interested neuroscientist Dr. Diane Powell of Medford, Oregon. Indeed, Dr. Powell is quoted as believing telepathy represents an alternative form of communication between autistic children and their parents, who desperately want to communicate with each other but cannot. Dr. Powell believes that if primary language is compromised, as happens in some forms of autism, telepathy can emerge. She claims to have seen telepathy in at least seven different people and dedicates her research time to the subject. As one of my professors on my dissertation committee told me one day, "If one brain demonstrates a behavior, it means the brain can do it."

According to Dr. Black, neurosurgeon, "The anatomy and biochemistry of the human brain is God's greatest art. It is quite simply the most beautiful structure in the known universe." Dr. Black articulates, "Whenever I look at the pathways and intricacies of the human brain, I am looking at God's art. Every time I operate on the brain, it makes me more spiritual." While this level of spiritual connection between the brain and God may not be accepted or believed by all, it is worth thinking about, given the complexity of the brain and what it might represent beyond a random collection of cells.

Was the brain created as a means for humans to have the ability to consider the presence of God, to be spiritual, and to communicate with God? Might this be the answer to the question posed by this book, What is the purpose of my brain? Perhaps not, perhaps the brain is sheer chance, produced from genetic evolution with the sole purpose of thought, emotion, movement and limited by human life span. Certainly, the brain and its abilities have evolved to a more sophisticated state over our many years of existence, and very few would argue that the brain is not complicated.

Does the brain indeed have a more prominent or significant purpose—such as the appreciation and belief in a higher being or God, the creation of a consciousness or "other" that can witness our own being and make decisions and judgments of our own being, and maybe the derivation of an energy, spirit, or soul that lives beyond and is external to the physical structure of the body, thereby guaranteeing a connection to this or another universe even after the death of our body? Is this the purpose of our brain and, therefore, our opportunity to transcend, to rise above earthly limitation, and to remain connected forever? Is the brain involved in our salvation?

For me, the complexity of the brain and the fact that we really have very little understanding of what it does or, more importantly, what it can do tells me that the brain has a far greater role than simply being a conduit to thought, movement, and emotion. It is true that we should be in awe that emotion, thought, and movement are produced from a complicated interaction of neurons, blood, oxygen, glucose, lipid, hormones, and chemicals. However, it makes perfect sense to me that a system as complicated as the human brain would have a greater role, something more profound, and extending beyond our inner workings and current understanding. It also is of interest to me to ask why a system so complicated would not have the ability to fix or heal itself, or other parts of the body for that matter. Perhaps it does, and we simply do not know how yet. One day, we will know how to tap into this energy source known as the human brain, and things that now seem impossible or silly will become a reality.

Indeed, sometimes the silliness sneaks through the cracks of our rather closed view of life, and we are forced to sit and ponder what something means or how something happens. At those moments, we might get a chill running through our body, as if someone or something has connected with us or has alerted us to a future or concurrent event. Consider those moments in your life from the perspective of this book and be open to the potential that there exists a dynamic energy ongoing inside and around us and that perhaps the brain was given so that we could connect, interact, and be guided by such energies.

Rhythms and the Brain

We arrive in the world bathed in the warmth of our mother's womb, listening to the music of her voice, and the rhythm of her heartbeat. This is significant since these are the earliest inputs and influences to the brain. These are important, if not critical, to early shaping of our brains and to a foundational need of the brain that I refer to as *neural rhythm*. Rhythms of life and the balance it generates offer us the peace from whence we came. Our challenge in life is to find the rhythms that surround us, the neural rhythms our brain seeks, and connect with them.

As I write this part of the book, I am sitting at a table in the Outer Banks, enjoying a family vacation. I look away from my computer screen and scan the grand vista of the

Atlantic Ocean (see Appendix 2). The majesty of the ocean with so much water demands that we consider how and why. Great questions with no clear answers, but I tend to think that the greater forces and energies I have talked about are in play here. Some may believe an ocean is random or chance, but not me. Complex things require intent; and because there are a variety of complex things such as the brain, universe, and nature, I tend to think intent far outweighs random as the explanation for existence and purpose of such complexity. I also tend to believe that the complexity does not exist in isolation but rather integrates into an even grander unity, one that can be connected on a spiritual and energy medium.

I walked the beach each morning on my family vacation, and I have indeed been blessed to visit many beaches in the world (see Appendix 2). Each visit to the shore is quite special, filled with immediate reflection, meditation, and humility. The ocean provides never-ending waves—wave after wave smashing into the shore, creating a sound that is predictable and calming and provides a natural rhythm, a neural rhythm. I find it more than curious that humans save money for an entire year and plan time in their busy schedules to get back to the ocean in order to return to the rhythm that our brains (we) so desperately desire and need.

Each evening, whether the sky is clear or not, we are bombarded by the vast wonder and beauty of thousands of stars, sometimes planets, and even the Milky Way. On a clear night, this will cause all of us to sit in awe and respect the power that surrounds us: the rhythm to the life of nature at night. Stars emerge each night just as the sun rises and sets each day. Our entire natural existence is framed from the perspective of rhythms, and our brain needs such rhythm to generate balance and peace. It is our daily life itself that ignores this and seduces us to leave the path of neural rhythm for the path of technologies, rapid living, and task completion. This only leads to acute and chronic stress, inflammation, worry, psychological and emotional turmoil, and a damaged immune system.

I believe the universe and the great powers and spiritual energy that lie external to our bodies also are built from and require rhythm. The sun rises and sets, the stars emerge each night, the wind blows, the seasons come and go, the sun provides light and warmth, the moon is always watching, and the waves simply keep coming. The Milky Way contains a set number of planets surrounded by moons set within a larger universe with more galaxies and solar systems—all that seem to have a place, a natural rhythm.

Living in the Northeast, I fully appreciate the seasons. I spent nearly ten years in Tucson in the earlier part of my life, so I have become rather weak with winter weather. Seasons are part of our existence, and they are predictably consistent in their rhythm. I observe as the summer provides warmth and blue sky and the opportunity to enjoy activities outside the home. Summer invites fall to the stage and the beauty of trees changing color and then leaves falling to the ground.

The air chills, and the wind seems to begin to take on a more assertive, if not aggressive, tone. This alerts all of us to what is coming in the form of cold, snow, sleet, and ice. Some people love this season, but as I noted, I will be the one in the corner, cowering!

Snow falls in large flakes and seems to just keep coming day after day. The winds howl, and most of us tend to get beat up a bit as the winter season extends beyond several months. Animals are well aware of this season, and they too know to prepare far in advance to their need to move or burrow to survive. With great relief, some of us welcome with a big smile the introduction of spring. Rain arrives, but the temperature moderates. The remnants of winter fade, offering a fresh air that seems to bring life back to our psyche. The animals begin to reemerge, and our new cycle of life begins. These seasons, with all the psychology wrapped up into them, just keep coming in a consistency that is rhythmical. I find this interesting and wonder why. Is it simply about gravitational pull and the earth's movement on its axis? Perhaps, but perhaps there is more.

The author of the human brain and the universe sprinkled a heavy dose of rhythm into our existence, world, and DNA. Why is rhythm so important? Perhaps we seek a return to the womb of our mother where the most nurturing environment for rhythm, warmth, and peace exists. Perhaps God understands the importance of rhythm and balance to any system, small or large, which some refer to as homeostasis and regularity. Our brain rejoices when rhythms are found that align our electrical and chemical being and yield a sense of peace and balance, a feeling that all is right. I tend to think nature and the universe also rejoice in the balance and peace brought to their existence from rhythms. Sometimes we humans capture such a moment of peace and balance, and we can appreciate how right it feels. Neural rhythms are real and are needed, and if we are open to the energies inside and outside of our organism, we can immerse ourselves in such rhythms and rejoice in the peace that results.

If God is indeed the author of our brain as He made us in his image, He most certainly had a reason for giving us a brain. The next chapter will turn to the Gospel according to John to try and discover clues suggested by the teachings of Christ that might help us better understand his purpose for giving us a brain. (Near the time of his death, Jesus told John to accept his mother as his own, and he told his mother to take John as her son—this seems to provide reasonable support to John knowing Jesus well and to being a credible source for this book.)

6

Where Do I Turn?
Can the Bible Help?

I am the way, the truth, and the life; no one
comes to my Father but through me.

—John 14:5

By asking the foundational question, What is the purpose of my brain? I quickly realized I was not going to find the answer in my traditional texts from the neurosciences. I began to read basic material in quantum physics (Zohar 1990), which was quite interesting, regarding how atomic energy can connect and affect another regardless of the distance that separates two distinct entities. This helped to suggest a mechanical explanation for my thoughts on neural energy and the mechanism by which we might be able to affect our internal organism, affect others around us, and connect with the greater universe. This perspective was provided additional support by a recent publication in nature (Henson et al. 2015), which supports what is known as *spooky action at a distance*, in which manipulating one object instantaneously seems to affect another far away in an inherent part of the quantum world. If atomic matter in an object can be influenced via the manipulation of atomic matter in another object that exists at a distinct place so that these properties of different objects become "entangled," it raises the question of whether humans, also composed of atomic matter, can affect other humans at distant places.

Some (Graziano 2010) have posited that the experience of self, soul, consciousness, and all that occupies or represents the spiritual world is a perception of mind and is created by a social machinery of the brain. Similarly, there is some thought that the brain invented or created God rather than the other way around (Naskar 2015). Still others remain in the more traditional brain-behavior realm, explaining the neural circuitry of mindfulness (Hanson and Mendius 2009), structural changes that occur in the brain with deep meditation or prayer (Newberg and Waldman 2010), or the growing relationship between prayer, forgiveness, love, and health (Koenig 1999; Hill 2009; Siegel 2002). Each of these is a fascinating read written by neuroscientists and clinicians who teach us about the power of the brain and how the brain responds to spiritual and emotional energy. Perhaps pushing our imagination even further toward my own interests in the spiritual energy and power of the brain are two books by Haggerty (2009) and Hamilton (2009). Despite these important contributions and the fascinating questions raised in these books, I continue to search for the answer to my own question, What is the purpose of my brain?

Rosie Hill wrote a text on *Neurotheology Reveals the Covert Bondage of Unforgiveness (2009)* in which she describes how God created the anatomical regions of the human cortex and our ability to free ourselves from negative feelings by the power of forgiveness. This text moved directly to the impact God has on the brain and behavior, at least in terms of forgiveness.

The human brain is far too complicated for neuroscience to explain or understand at the current time. While neuroscience has moved our understanding of the brain and the processes of the brain forward in dramatic fashion over the past twenty years, we remain rather primitive. We know there are neurochemicals, but we do not know how many exist or precisely how they work. We know how the basic mechanics of communication between brain cells occur, but we do not understand how or why abnormalities occur in such communication. We do not understand completely how complex functions of memory, forgetting, planning, dreaming, imagination, or consciousness work. There remains debate even today about the differences between brain and mind.

Our brain's capacity is likely unlimited, yet we do not understand this, and we even begin to feel awkward by merely suggesting that the brain has the ability to heal the body. We do know the brain is affected and shaped by environmental input, and we know we experience things that are described as odd or miraculous because we cannot explain them. We have the ability to process and perceive our internal condition and the world around us. We even have the ability to ponder about great and majestic things such as the stars in the sky. We have the ability to believe in a higher being, heaven, and we fully appreciate right from wrong. These are only a few examples of how incredibly complex and brilliant the human brain is, regardless of our inability to explain it.

The brain also contains our identity, our ability to witness or view ourselves as if we are third party to ourselves. We are able to contemplate, commit to, or refute God and to understand our position on earth and a place called heaven. It is true that the human brain may be within our heads specifically to conduct these tasks, these behaviors, and that is it. This seems to me, however, to be a rather limited and finite reason for having a central nervous system.

I have another thought that the brain serves a greater purpose, one that enables each of us to connect with ourselves, with others, and with our universe. My idea suggests that the brain was granted us in order to serve as a conduit to commune with our universe and the God that created both. In essence, the brain is a conduit for us to relate to God as he intended and to appreciate all the majesty that surrounds us (see Appendix 2). It is from the brain provided us by God that things such as forgiveness, prayer, meditation, and love can be healing in ways the authors cited above wrote about in their books. Perhaps it is the brain that is the conduit to the Holy Spirit that scripture teaches us is everlasting, and that underlies some of the "miracles" that we hear about and the stories of peace that live on after death of the body. The Spirit expressed via the brain as granted by God may be the energy medium by which we remain connected to our universe with a feeling of "heaven" after the earthly structure of our body dies.

These are some heavy thoughts I am presenting, and I realize I may not be the first to have the curiosity about the role of the brain and such matters of God. Regardless, I know I must turn to scripture for possible clues that might support my argument that the human brain is created and granted us by God as an energy medium and conduit to heal and balance within, to interact and shape without, to remain connected with the energy sources of the universe, to remain connected in a spiritual presence beyond the life of the body, and to ultimately commune with God. If we are to believe in the Christian faith and about life everlasting and the role that the Holy Spirit plays in this experience, it seems logical to me to explore the role of the human brain as it is our energy source and the only system in our body that feels, thinks, and experiences in ways we do not even understand.

7

Lessons from Scripture

I am turning to the Bible—both a Catholic version and the King James Version, and specifically to the Gospel according John to help guide me, to provide me some education on matters of the Holy Spirit—and to scripture that might connect to the thesis of this book. As I noted above, I am not an expert on Christianity or any religion. I am a follower of Christ with tremendous faith and an obsessive curiosity about the brain and the purpose for humans having a brain. From these writings, we might be able to glean the components of a connection from God to us and, more importantly, to our brain as our own grand processor of these teachings. In the book of John, apostle of Jesus, I am struck by his frequent use of the word *light*:

> There was a man named John sent by God who came as a witness to testify to the *light* so that through him all men might believe—but only to testify to the *light*, for he himself was not the *light*. The real *light* which gives *light* to every man was coming into the world. (John 1:6–9, italics added)

In this passage from the apostle John, the word *light* seems to refer to God and to the Holy Spirit as he describes the "real light giving light to every man." In a sense, the word *light* is used as a noun and an active verb that can be given from God to man. These words are important since we read them even today, over two thousand years from their writing, and humans continue to relate to them. My interest in this passage deals with an inherent question, Where is the *light* to be received, felt, or processed by man so that man knows he has received it? For that matter, what is the system that enables man to "know"?

John's writings focus on the Holy Spirit, which can be interpreted to be a dynamic energy form of God and manifestation of God. According to the apostle John (ch. 1, vv. 32–33) in his description of John the Baptist:

> John gave his testimony also: I saw the Spirit descend like a dove from the sky and it came to rest on him. But I did not recognize him. The one who sent me to baptize with water told me, when you see the Spirit descend and rest on someone, it is he who is to baptize

with the Holy Spirit. Now I have seen for myself and
have testified, this is God's chosen one.

John the Baptist saw the Spirit descend, and he testified
he did not recognize. The ability to see and to recognize are
well-established functions (sensory and visual perception)
of the brain. John then related a memory regarding what he
was told, and he was able to comprehend from the memory
what the meaning of his sighting was. Once again, memory
and visual perception and comprehension are functions of
the brain. In seemingly direct terms, John the Baptist was
describing his experience of what was going on around him,
how it was related directly to what he was told by the Holy
Spirit, and what his comprehension and interpretation of
this was. His brain was the conduit from God via the Holy
Spirit to not only understand what was happening in front of
him but to then communicate it to others. This is a concrete
example of a spiritual energy (Holy Spirit) communing with
a human brain that then enables the brain to feel and behave
(neural energy).

John the Baptist had to have a system within him to
accomplish all these rather complicated behaviors, feelings,
and interpretation/communication of events. The system
was his brain, and since scripture teaches that John was a
messenger called to do certain things and to teach certain
things in anticipation of the spiritual and bodily arrival of
God, it is reasonable to suggest that the human brain was

granted by God in order to encode, experience, and share God's message.

In John's writings (ch. 3, vv. 1–8), he describes an interesting interchange between Jesus and Nicodemus, who was a Pharisee or member of the Jewish leadership. Nicodemus was confused by Jesus' words that he would raise up a temple in three days if it were destroyed. Nicodemus asked Jesus, "How can a man be born again once he is old? Can he return to his mother's womb and be born over again?" Jesus responded in a way that distinguishes earthly bound matters from the Spirit: "I solemnly assure you, no one can enter into God's kingdom without being begotten of water and Spirit. Flesh begets flesh, Spirit begets Spirit." Jesus continued, "The wind blows where it will. You hear the sound it makes, but you do not know where it comes from, or where it goes. So it is with everyone begotten of the Spirit."

This is an indication that Jesus, Son of God, distinguishes earthly bound things, such as the body, from heavenly things, such as the Holy Spirit. Further, Jesus taught that for those who are open to the Holy Spirit, they will experience everlasting life even though the body is dead. Energy in the form of the Holy Spirit sent by God to humans who have faith in him is active and everlasting.

Where is the Holy Spirit felt, processed, and followed? It must be the human brain; and because the Holy Spirit is so important and emphasized in the teachings of Jesus, it is reasonable to speculate that the brain has a critical purpose, perhaps the most critical purpose of all: dealing with faith and everlasting life. If the Holy Spirit can be considered an energy-based representation of God, the brain is also considered an energy source and a natural conduit for the flow and experience of spiritual energy in this case between God and human. It might be the reason God gave us our brain so that we were made in his image.

In perhaps one of the most cited verses of any kind in the history of the written word, John describes Jesus' teachings to Nicodemus: "Yes, God so loved the world that he gave his only Son, that whoever believes in him may not die, but rather have eternal life" (John 3:16). This passage requires close inspection for our interest in exploring the purpose of our brain. Jesus states that God loved the world, and in this case, it probably is safe to infer that *world* means "earth" since the use of the word *whoever* infers "human." The use of the word *believes* is critical as, again, the human requires a system that can actually believe, and that has to be the brain.

A major tenet of Christianity is belief or faith, and it demands the presence of a brain to express or feel belief or faith. The teaching from Christ also is the first in the book of John to express "eternal life." Jesus describes to Nicodemus the idea of not dying but of having eternal life. Here again, Jesus is referring to a spiritual existence that is bound to him and that through faith, we humans have the ability to exist eternally. If the Spirit is what actually has eternal life, I believe it is fair to suggest that the brain is needed to receive the

Spirit to act in ways that express faith and to even experience, from a spiritual basis, "eternal life." Looking at this line of argument another way, can any of this be possible without the brain? My answer to that is yes since God can do all things. However, I am still asserting that the brain was and is God's intention and creation so that the critical behaviors necessary for "eternal life" can be learned, felt, understood, and practiced by mortal man. The brain is also the miracle system given us by God to actually vie for and experience a spiritual life that can be "eternal."

These words from Jesus on eternal life and the relationship of his body and blood to eternal life are difficult to understand, and the same was true when it was originally spoken by Christ, at least according to the Gospel of John (ch. 6, vv. 60–64):

> After hearing his words, many of his disciples remarked: This sort of talk is hard to endure. How can anyone take it seriously? Jesus was fully aware that his disciples were murmuring in protest at what he had said. Does it shake your faith Jesus asked them? What then if you were to see the son of man ascend to where he was before? It is the Spirit that gives life; the flesh is useless. The words I spoke to you are the Spirit and life. Yet among you there are some who do not believe.

The point of emphasis for me in this passage is Jesus's statement that it is the Spirit that gives life and the flesh is useless. This is a common teaching of Christ that emphasizes the Spirit and deemphasizes the body or flesh. He further asserts that his words "are the Spirit and life." This suggests that our openness to his words enables the Spirit to enter and facilitates our belief, our faith, which is the pathway to salvation, to eternal life. This is critical since all aspects of this premise (pathway to salvation) necessitates the human brain since it is from the brain that we can be open, hear, comprehend, receive the Holy Spirit, feel the Holy Spirit, and have the faith necessary to receive and believe in eternal life.

Jesus also describes an early example of the power of *neural plasticity* when he declares, "The words I spoke to you are the Spirit and life." Since he also stated, "It is the Spirit that gives life, the flesh is useless," we can infer that his words shaped the brain in an active way and enabled a spiritual-based life that was not of the body or flesh and that facilitated eternal life. The processing of his words, the idea that there is a spiritual existence distinct of the body that is of greater value, and that the Spirit is everlasting further indicates the need for a system to facilitate these things. The human brain processes words and language, perceives the difference between physical and spiritual, and can appreciate the teachings that faith in Christ as the Son of God is necessary to gain eternal life, a life that is spiritual in nature.

In yet another example of Jesus's teaching of faith and life everlasting, John (ch. 11, vv. 25–26) describes Jesus's words to Martha, sister of Lazarus who had just died: "I am the resurrection and the life: whoever believes in me, though he should die, will come to life; and whoever is alive and believes in me will never die."

I use this passage to again underscore the importance placed on a distinction that is repeated throughout the Bible between the body, which has a time and earthbound limitation, and a spiritual existence, which is potentially eternal. The eternal life comes from belief in Christ; and the action of belief, being a cognitive process, falls to the brain.

Summary

Certainly, the Bible is far too expansive for the purposes of this book. I chose to focus on the Gospel according to John in order to generate thematic consistent teachings of Christ that might help in answering my question about the purpose of my brain. In review of John's Gospel, there are indeed consistent themes in the teachings of Christ that offer insight into the purpose of my brain:

- Jesus uses the word *light* multiple times to describe himself or his presence. He also uses the word *light* in a manner that can be given to another; in this case, God giving light to man. The use of the word *light* seems to take on a spiritual essence as well since it is given to man as a manifestation of God.
- The concept of Spirit is critical as Jesus repeats the importance of the Holy Spirit in his teachings and the idea that the Spirit is what gives life, not the flesh.

- Jesus teaches a distinction between a spiritual life and existence and a more earthbound flesh or body life. He underscores the value of the spiritual over the body.
- Jesus describes the pathway to eternal life, which is a spiritual existence, by having faith and a belief in Jesus as the Son of God.
- Jesus describes that it is possible for man to receive the Holy Spirit.
- Jesus told his disciples that his words are the Spirit and life. I consider words to be neurochemical activators, and Jesus's words continue to have a direct effect on our brain, neurochemistry, and behavior.
- The Spirit was described as descending and as seen by John the Baptist, indicating that the spiritual energy from God is dynamic and active. From the teachings of Christ as written by John in his Gospel, it is clear that a cognitive, perceptual, and even sensory capacity is required for humans to understand, follow, and adhere to the teachings of Christ, which enables eternal life. Examples of this include John the Baptist "testifying to," "seeing," "not recognizing," and then comprehending from memory of what he was "told"—all of which required his brain.

Jesus reiterates a distinction between earth or flesh, which is transient and finite, with the infinite and eternal Spirit of heaven and God. The teachings of everlasting life, presence of God within humans, and being one with God all seem to coalesce around a spiritual essence, the Holy Spirit. This is a difficult concept to understand; and even the disciples, according to John, did not understand this teaching. Our *difficulty* in understanding and our *desire* to *understand*, to *follow* the path for living a spiritual life, to remain faithful to Christ all for an opportunity for everlasting life demands the presence of a brain, a central nervous system.

It is clear there was not only an active interaction between Jesus, his followers, and detractors during his life on earth; there was also a repeated teaching by Jesus of the spiritual essence of who he was and who his Father was and how humans can be open to, access, and live a life filled with this Spirit. It seems as though Christ was laying out the lesson plan, the strategy, with all the critical parts for humans to both learn and follow during their time on earth in order to achieve eternal life beyond earth. All of this interaction necessitates each human to have a processing system to sense, learn, comprehend, behave, and ultimately believe with unending faith so that the spiritual eternal life that Christ described could be obtained. It also seems both reasonable and necessary to assert that our brain was granted us to communicate reciprocally with the Spirit, to seek guidance, and to feel the love of Jesus.

While no conclusion can be drawn, it seems fair to suggest that Christ was teaching, which means humans were learning and then behaving in supportive ways or otherwise. Certainly, Christ was eventually executed, indicating that some were not supportive of his teachings. From the perspective of the brain, humans were and continue to process Christ's teachings using their brain, and this led to particular outcomes: some became devout followers; others executed him. Jesus taught consistently the need to believe, to have faith, to lead a life of love and forgiveness, and to follow him. As humans, we only have one system that can accomplish these cognitive, emotional, and motor functions—and that is the brain!

On the surface, this seems rather elementary. Christ is teaching humans, and of course, humans are going to use their brains to process and react. This is abundantly true even today, over two thousand years after the death of Jesus. However, my intent in writing this book is to take a deeper dive! If Christ is the Son of God and Savior of the world as I believe, and he made humans in his image, he knew what was needed in order to have interaction and to relate to us in a way that taught us forever the path necessary for eternal life.

That is the point of this text: that this is not all random, that Christ created humans in his image to include a brain, a system capable of interacting with him, of communicating with him, of comprehending his message, and of receiving and living a spiritual life given us by his Holy Spirit so that we may obtain salvation in an eternal life. In this case, *eternal life* means a spiritual eternal communion with God, one that outlives the earthbound flesh and body and where we feel the infinite power of his love. It is the brain that experiences his warmth, his love, his light, and the words he described as "the Spirit and life." Perhaps the purpose of my brain is not simply to learn and to behave. Perhaps the purpose of my brain is to *be open to the lessons and path set for us by Christ* so that we can achieve salvation, an eternal spiritual connection and unity with all that is good.

Our Neurospiritual Path
The Greatest Medicine
Lies within You

What is the Purpose of My Brain?

 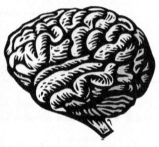

8

Neural Energy:
Spiritual Healing of Self

More precious than gold is health and wellbeing, no
treasure greater than a healthy body, no happiness,
than a joyful heart. Preferable is death to a bitter life,
unending sleep to constant illness. Do not give in to
sadness, torment not yourself with brooding. Gladness
of heart is the very life of man, cheerfulness prolongs
his days. Distract yourself, renew your courage, drive
resentment far away from you; For worry has brought
death to many, nor is there aught to be gained from
resentment. Envy and anger shorten one's life, worry
brings on premature old age; One who is cheerful
and gay at his table benefits from his food.

—Sirach 30:14–25

It is fair to say that Americans are expert at feeling, producing, and sharing stress. According to the National Institute of Mental Health, anxiety disorders are a serious medical illness that affects at least nineteen million American adults. There are many more who experience fear and mild nervousness on a daily basis. At my Brain Health Center (www.brainhealthctr.com) located in a lovely northern suburb of Pittsburgh, the most common struggle our guests arrive with is anxiety. There is no common profile, and we only see those who have the courage and insight to seek assistance. But it is also fair to say that anxiety does not discriminate and will affect nearly all of us at one time or another. For those with chronic anxiety, life can be quite challenging, and it can indeed limit one's life in ways that are problematic.

The Anxiety and Depression Association of America (ADAA [www.adaa.org]) report anxiety and depression to be the most common mental illness in the United States, affecting forty million adults age eighteen and older (18 percent of the population). Generalized anxiety disorder (GAD) affects 6.8 million adults or 3.1 percent of the US population, with women being affected twice as likely as men. Other forms of anxiety are also quite common and listed below:

Anxiety	Subtype Number Affected	% of Population
Panic disorder	6 million	2.7% (women > men)
Social anxiety disorder	15 million	6.8% (gender equality)

Specific phobia	19 million	8.7 % (women > men)
Obsessive-compulsive disorder	2.2 million	1.0% (gender equality)
Post-traumatic stress disorder	7.7 million	3.5% (women > men)

Anxiety disorders are highly treatable, but it is estimated that only one-third of those suffering receive treatment. A study commissioned by the ADAA (Greenberg et al. 1999) reports that anxiety disorders cost the United States more than forty-two billion dollars annually, which occupies a significant amount of the total economic output for mental health expenditures. More than twenty billion of these costs are related to repeated use of health-care services—people with anxiety disorders who seek relief for symptoms that mimic physical illness. Indeed, people with anxiety disorder are three to five times more likely to go to the doctor and six times more likely to be hospitalized for psychiatric disorders than those who do not suffer anxiety.

It is common for those with anxiety disorder to also be diagnosed with major depression. Nearly 50 percent of those diagnosed with depression are also diagnosed with an anxiety disorder according to ADAA. Major depressive disorder is the leading cause of disability in the United States for those ages fifteen to forty-four. Nearly fifteen million American adults (6.7 percent of US population) over the age of eighteen are affected each year. Depression can occur at any age, but the median age at onset is 32.5, and it is more prevalent in women versus men.

While these statistics are primarily focused on adults, it is important to note that both anxiety and depression can affect children and older adults. Indeed, anxiety affects nearly one in eight children, and anxiety in older adults is as common as it is with adults. Depressive symptoms are much more common in older adults relative to younger adults even if full-blown major diagnostic depression is not. Residential setting also influences one's mood with increased levels of depression noted in hospitals and nursing homes relative to home.

Unfortunately, depression and anxiety, as well as all types of mental illness, are not specific to the United States. Rather, mental illness is a worldwide problem. According to the Centers for Disease Control and Prevention (CDC) and World Health Organization (WHO), depression was the third most important cause of disease burden in 2004. Depression was less of a burden in less economically advanced nations, but first in middle- to high-income countries. Anxiety disorders were rated as the most common class of mental disorders present in the general population, and again, a higher prevalence is noted in developed versus nondeveloped nations. Women outnumber men in cases of depression and anxiety worldwide.

Alzheimer's disease is the sixth leading cause of death in the United States and affects nearly 5.2 million Americans. This number, as well as the 46 million who suffer the disease worldwide, will swell in the next several decades, causing enormous psychological, physical, emotional, and financial burden to families and nations (CDC). To date, we have no cure or prevention for Alzheimer's or the many other types of irreversible dementias. There are so many other conditions, problems, and afflictions of the brain and spirit that I cannot list them in this book. Suffice it to say that we humans are not perfect, and unfortunately, we suffer many different types of illnesses.

This overview is the typical manner in which a clinician presents information. I provided statistics on clinical disorders and attempted to illustrate how pervasive each is in the general population and even informed you on differences in prevalence rates by gender and age. While this is important, I fear it misses the bigger issue that this book is attempting to address: What about the human condition? And is it true that if one is not diagnosed with a particular condition, one is not suffering? My contention is that humans live and exist on a continuum of well-being and you-can-name-the-condition-of-interest, such as anxiety or depression. And everyone can be placed on that continuum. It is not accurate to divide the human race into those who are depressed or anxious and those who are not. This is how the medical or clinical profession views the world. I believe a far more accurate view of the world is to try and understand what humans experience and to empower them with the knowledge of how to build balance and peace in their lives. This is not a clinical perspective but, rather, a means of improving the human condition, and I believe we all come equipped to improve and heal the self.

This brings us back to my concept of neural energies and the empowerment we have to shape our brains through something known as *neural plasticity*. This is not a new concept, but it has regained a great resurgence because of recent findings from neuroscience. Our brains can be shaped all across the life span because they are dynamic, constantly reorganizing, and malleable. The brain is always seeking input to process, to be stimulated by, and to then share with the world. It turns out that environmental input that is "novel and complex" (Nussbaum 2003) has a health benefit to the brain as it helps the brain build "brain resilience" (Wilson 2011) that occurs at the cellular level. Your brain can also be influenced by your own thoughts and by what you do, such as mental stimulation, physical exercise, good nutrition, socialization, and spiritual activities (Nussbaum 2011; see fig. 1).

We learned earlier of Jesus's message and his words that contained the Spirit for everlasting life, perhaps one of the earliest examples of neural plasticity because of how his words shaped the brains and lives of those who demonstrated faith in him. Further, your brain is shaped by relationships, by information you process, by nature, by powers and spiritual energies that exist around us, and by God, who made us in his image. The fact that our brain has plasticity is a tremendous gift and further supports my belief that we are connected to ourselves, to others around us, and to the natural and spiritual energy of the universe. It is the brain that serves as the conduit to this connection. This chapter is about one of the powers we have, which is to shape our brains internally and, therefore, our bodies using our neural energy.

By turning to scripture (Matthew 17:19–21), we again might draw some lessons from the teachings of Jesus regarding our (human) power to heal. Upon not being able to heal a boy who was described by his father as demented, Jesus's disciples came to Jesus and asked, "Why could we not expel the demon?" Jesus replied, "Because you have so little trust. I assure you if you had faith the size of a mustard seed, you would be able to say to this mountain, 'Move from here to there,' and it would move. Nothing would be impossible for you."

In yet another teaching (Luke 17:17–19), Jesus cured ten lepers, yet only one returned to him to praise and give thanks to him. Jesus replied, "Were not all ten made whole? Where are the other nine? Was there no one to return and give thanks to God except this foreigner?" He said to the man, "Stand up and go your way. Your faith has been your salvation."

Throughout the New Testament, there are stories describing miracles of Jesus healing the blind, the crippled, lepers, and others. When asked for how this can happen, Jesus turns to the person's faith in him and God as the answer. For purposes of this book and this chapter, a person's faith is a cognitive and spiritual function that has an ability to heal within. Indeed, according to Jesus, pure faith has no limits to its power.

Perhaps the most powerful example of this can be found in John 11:1–43, when Jesus raised Lazarus from the dead. In this passage, Jesus told Martha, sister of Lazarus, "I am the resurrection and the life; whoever believes in me though he should die, will come to life; and whoever is alive and believes in me will never die." Jesus asked Martha if she believed this, and she replied, "Yes, Lord, I have come to believe that you are the Messiah, the Son of God: he who is to come into the world." Jesus than proceeded to approach where Lazarus was raised, and he asked his Father to give him the power to bring life back to Lazarus.

It is of interest that throughout the New Testament, Jesus performed miracles so that people would believe that he was the Son of God. Jesus asked others, including his own disciples, whether they had faith in him and even who the people said that he was. In Matthew 16:13–19, Peter answered, "You are the Messiah, the son of the living God." Jesus responded to Peter by saying, "Blest are you Simon, son of John, no mere man has revealed this to you, but my heavenly Father. You are the rock and on this rock I will build my church and the jaws of death shall not prevail against it."

Faith and belief in God and therefore ourselves is paramount to our (human) ability to affect change within and beyond ourselves. Faith and belief are indeed functions of the brain, so again, it would seem reasonable that God provided us a brain so that we might have the opportunity to express and to live a life dedicated to such faith and belief.

It is from this faith and belief that we might heal within and help others to heal, even maintain power over nature itself. I refer to such energy or spiritual power as neural energy, and this chapter is dedicated to understanding that we have such power and that, when practiced and applied, we can bring health and healing to our being.

> Have no anxiety at all, but in everything, by prayer and petition, with thanksgiving, make your requests known to God. (Philippians 4:6)

Humans and Balance

Similar to our brain's need for rhythms, we also seek balance in our lives. One of the reasons anxiety and depression are so prevalent in American society is the fact that our culture breeds imbalance. We move too fast, are too heavily tasked with deadlines, process too much information in the digital age, and do not sleep enough. We literally do not know how to relax, how to give ourselves time and space with *digital-free zones*. In short, our brains have very little, if any, balance.

The concept of being out of balance is not easily understood. Indeed, there are many ways to lose balance. Similar to falling from tripping or from weakness in a lower limb, which can cause loss of balance, our emotional and mental energy systems can become imbalanced. As discussed earlier in this book, our brains were developed from rhythms provided by our mother while we were in her womb. These rhythms forged a core ingredient to overall balance where our emotional system aligns with our analytic, causing a wonderful fusion for calm, stillness, and inner peace. Unfortunately, balance takes conscious effort for most of us, and there is direct competition with the task-oriented, fast-paced, and demanding society where we live that results in our brains being imbalanced.

Balance?

The American culture has seen an explosion of mindfulness-based interventions and exercises to try and address the unfortunate reality that we Americans are stressed out of our minds! There are books (Newberg and Waldman

2010; Hanson and Mendius 2009), workshops, DVDs, retreats, and podcasts to help teach us about stress and how to relax. I am concerned by a rapid eruption of big-business products being sold on the market with exaggerated promises to vulnerable Americans—creams, pills, vitamins, exercise equipment, supplements, diets, etc., that carry promises for this or that. I often ask my audiences, What are you searching for? What is missing? And why do you think the missing piece can be bought? For me, this searching represents a somewhat sad state of affairs because so many people seem to have lost an understanding that the balance and peace they are searching for can be captured by introspection, exploration, and understanding of self and the utilization of their spiritual power. The difficulty of such an approach to a type of enlightenment is that it is not easy and certainly not quick. There is no product that will fill the void in one's life, that which is missing. Often the missing part is something personal and related to our gestalt as a person and our identity. Much like our dismay if we were missing a limb, a fragmented emotional, spiritual, or psychological identity can result in imbalance, unease, and feelings of not being whole.

We do possess the ability, the power, and spiritual energy to connect with our internal being to not only identify areas of physical and emotional tension but to allocate our thinking and mental energy to reduce and even rid ourselves of such imbalance. This is likely the message Jesus taught us so many years ago when he spoke to us about the power of faith to heal us. While many schools of meditation and mindfulness can teach a variety of techniques on how to focus and be present, the fundamental and critical point is that we do possess an innate power within our brain to both harness and allocate neural energy to help heal within. We do have the neuroanatomy and neurophysiology to be mindful and to gain balance. We can generate a focused mental channeling of energy to points in our body or virtual psyche that are not in sync or in balance.

There is indeed a need for heightened consciousness, awareness, and belief in one's neural energy to be successful at healing within—and yes, daily practice is required. For most, these are foreign concepts, but it is good to always remember the power of the brain and how it is an energy source that manages the homeostasis of our entire body. The brain produces and expresses an energy and spiritual power that directs thoughts and feelings throughout our body, resulting in emotional and psychological end points. Our ability to control and to guide such neural energy represents a new approach to personal health and well-being.

I also want to emphasize that being present may not always be very therapeutic or the particular point in time for one to be. Time is a continuum and not discrete. There are many variations of the past, present, and future. The good news is our brain has the ability to appreciate all. The frontal lobe provides us a sense of time estimation (know anybody in the family who is always late?) and the miracle to predict the future or at least plan for it. Our temporal lobes provide us with memory, and memories get tagged with emotional valence, personal priority, and time position on the continuum of our life.

If there is a magical moment you have experienced, being present is great. The memory of the event, however, can always enable you to be present in that magical moment. That is the beauty and value of memory; it can always call up a moment or experience that has therapeutic value. I would argue that this represents an example of the power of living in the past! For some, the present is so fraught with trauma and distress that it is not good to be present. The brain even may split and repress such experiences and cause a type of emotional shock so one can cope. I would also argue that when the present is too traumatic, the past is not the only avenue for escape. The future is also available to our brains as a means of generating hope (see section on hope later in the book). My point in this paragraph is to challenge a bit the whole doctrine of being "present" as if that is the only point on our time continuum where we can find peace and balance. The exact opposite may be true, and your brain knows that. Indeed, Jesus taught us that by believing in his Word, our future salvation would be guaranteed and that this future can remove any anxiety of today. I suggest we work at focusing our neural energy to place us at a point on our time continuum where our brain's reward system (see fig. 3) is triggered and we fill up with euphoria and positive energy!

Taming Your Amygdala

Your amygdala is a wonderful, "almond-shaped" structure that lies next to your hippocampus (critical to memory and new learning), sitting in the medial section of your temporal lobes within what is known as the limbic system (see fig. 2). The amygdala interestingly is larger in the male brain.

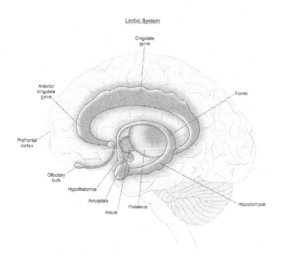

Figure 2. The amygdala and limbic system

Now, hundreds of thousands of years ago, it turns out that the amygdala was highly valuable because it provided the brain and, therefore, the body with an alert or warning that something was threatening. In those days, it tended to be a rather large animal that might have wanted to eat us! As such, the amygdala was and remains quite useful for survival. When the brain perceives a threat to our survival, the amygdala fires and causes a cascade of physiological changes in our brain and body.

One of the first things to occur is that the hypothalamic-pituitary-adrenal axis (HPA), which is related to our sympathetic (fight or flight) nervous system, is triggered. This sets off the release of neurochemicals and hormones that affect the physiology and function of our brain and body. For example, our brain releases norepinephrine while our adrenal glands located near our kidneys release adrenaline. In both cases, these cause our brain and body to get "amped up" as would be expected if we want to survive. Messages from the brain to the body include increase the heartbeat, expand the lungs for more oxygen, perfuse more blood to the thighs and biceps to prepare for combat or for flight, and shut off the digestive and reproductive systems. In short, we do not need to eat or engage in intimacy when we are about to be eaten!

One other interesting part of this reaction is that the hippocampus (slightly larger in women than men), located next to the amygdala (see fig. 2), is paused or reduced to a more limited capacity. This is likely related to survival and to our need to focus rather than learn new information. The limited hippocampal function means we do not learn or remember well when we are under stress. (Remember the test in school—did the answers come back to you after you left the stress-filled test room?)

This is precisely why a large number of people in their mid-fifties come to my office, worried they have Alzheimer's disease. I literally had to make a large copy of the illustration above that now sits in my office so that I can teach people what is happening in their brain and that their memory problems are due to poorly managed stress. The question I then pose to the person is, "What is chasing you? What is causing you to lose sleep at night?" Once we identify the stressor, we can work to quiet and tame the amygdala. Once that happens, our brain comes back to life and rejoices again.

Chronic stress—which can be defined as "a prolonged period of the changes in the brain and body," as I've described above—can cause damage to the hippocampus. We tend to see changes in the hippocampus with resulting memory deficit with veterans suffering Post Traumatic Stress Disorder (PTSD) as one example. The good news is that with proper care and nurturing environments, the brain can heal. That is why I included spirituality as one of the five major domains in my Brain Health Lifestyle® (Nussbaum 2010; see fig. 1). Research has taught us that proper breathing techniques practiced daily, progressive muscle relaxation practiced daily, meditation practiced daily, prayer on a daily basis, *digital-free zones* for your time, and interaction with nature around you (see Appendix 2) are excellent and natural ways to tame your amygdala and to bring balance to your brain and body. I tend to believe that Jesus's teachings of how we are to give away our possessions, not worry about money, not be bound to earthly matters, and instead to focus on our salvation through faith and love represented the *first lesson on taming our amygdala.*

The challenge within us on a daily basis is our ability to first recognize how balanced we are and then to manage the fast-paced, task-oriented American culture with our need to tame our amygdala. The good news is we are in control of what drives our inner workings, our homeostasis. Unfortunately, the rate of anxiety, depression, irritable bowel syndrome, headache, irritability, sleep disorder, ulcer, and relationship issues suggests many of us are not doing as well as we want.

From the time of the Bible, we were guided on ways to prioritize and to be freed of anxiety. I believe the reason why so many Americans exert such time and energy "searching" for that something to fill the void is really to rid anxiety and imbalance, and it serves as a mildly desperate desire for peace. An entire industry of products and services has emerged to try and fill this void, and Americans are responding. There is a positive to the "searching" because people are conscious of their feelings and unease. It is from the conscious that change can occur. Most are not even conscious of their inner feelings, psychology, and spiritual health; they simply know they are not sleeping and feeling "stressed."

This book underscores my belief that the power to heal lies within you and, more specifically, within your brain in the form of neural energy and a spiritual force granted us by Jesus. The message or thought originating from our brain forms an intention, a blueprint that the rest of the body follows.

This is critical, particularly when you consider our "will to live" as such a blueprint will direct the rest of the body to fight and live! We do indeed have the ability to be miserable, anxious, and out of balance, and this is the path so many have as a default. Fortunately, we have the God-given ability to be at peace, to be with balance, and to be without significant worry. Directing our internal spiritual energy (neural energy) inward is a wonderful prescription and healing practice, but it requires we prioritize it as a critical part of our daily lifestyle and appreciate the control we have over much of what causes us imbalance. Recall, you are the primary sculptor of your brain, and through being conscious and persistent, you can work toward a healthy, balanced, and spiritual brain.

I encourage everyone today to make time and space for yourselves. I recommend thirty minutes a day for "you time." This is the period of the day when no tasks are involved, no pressure to complete anything, no deadlines. This is your time to just be, to appreciate, to reflect, to forgive, and to pray. It is a wonderful time to meditate, to breathe, to relax your muscles, and to smile while feeling how good your body feels to smile. Open your arms wide as if all the little ones in your life want to hug you and close your eyes. Now smile and enjoy how you just sent positive and loving energy from your brain throughout your body. Make this you time a *digital-free zone* so outside noise will not interrupt your neural energy. Remember, you can place yourself along any part of your time continuum from wonderful experiences in the past to the present to speaking with God about your future. You are guiding your internal God-given Spirit expressed as neural energy inward, and this focus will guide the rest of the body to let go, to become vulnerable, and to be free emotionally from the things in life that seem so large yet are really small. You time is a priority, and I ask that you make it a priority in your life starting now.

9

Neural Energy:
Spiritual Healing of Others

Your brain does have the God-given energy and spiritual force to affect and even heal your internal organism. I have referred to this as neural energy in the book, and it has an enormous power for us to bring peace and balance into our lives. Indeed, this is the "medicine within" that I referred to earlier in this section of the book, and it was the focus of chapter 8. (It is critical to understand that the power to shape and to heal oneself, to bring peace and healing to others, and to commune with greater powers beyond us lies within each of us. We do not need to search for such power in products, liquids, foods, or pills any longer.)

Now I want to help everyone understand that your same spiritual energy, your neural energy, or "medicine within," has a similar positive and healing effect on others. Interestingly, our ability to bring good to others, to forgive, and to love is not only good and healthy for others; it is equally healthy for us! Can you name any man-made medicine that has the same ability?

There is a specific *reward system* in the brain that helps us appreciate pleasure, positive feelings, romance, and even deeper emotions such as love and joy (see fig. 3). It is a system directly related to love, sexual union, to the maternal behaviors associated with a mother viewing her baby's face, and child-rearing. I call this our *ahhhhh* experience, which can range from an orgasm to the wonderful feeling of the warm sun shining on our face on a calm and beautiful day. We engage this reward system when we care for ourselves and also when we care for others! It is also the area vulnerable to addiction and the sense of euphoria one reports when using cocaine or other substances. Think about a few *ahhhhh* moments in your life, and when you do, the reward system in your brain will rev up!

Interestingly, this region of the brain involves multiple areas: the cortex (prefrontal and temporal-parietal junction) and subcortex, including the limbic system (see fig. 3), the same older and primitive region we reviewed earlier in the book. I find it quite interesting that some of our most core feelings and human needs are related to this region of the brain, which developed long before the cortex. As such, our brain has a set of old neural systems and related chemicals and hormones that enable positive feelings, pleasure, romance, love, joy, forgiveness, and many other such emotions. What a great benefit if we only use it!

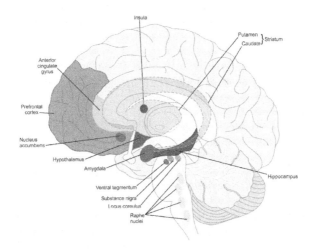

Figure 3: The reward system

Structures of our reward system particularly important for experience of positive feelings include the *hypothalamus*, *ventral tegmental area*, ventral pallidum, insula, putamen, amygdala, and nucleus accumbens (see fig. 3). Each of these structures forms a complicated reward-and-pleasure system that is influenced by chemicals such as *dopamine* (hypothalamus), *norepinephrine* (locus coeruleus), and *serotonin* (raphe nuclei) (see fig. 3). Interestingly, when we experience pleasure and positive feelings, our dopamine surges while serotonin is reduced in output. The latter can result in obsessive-compulsive behavior often related to new romance and love. In addition, *oxytocin, vasopressin* (produced in the hypothalamus and stored and released from the pituitary gland into the blood system), the *human growth hormone*, and even *testosterone* facilitate feelings of love, calm, peace and solidify bonding and long-standing affection between two people (Zeki 2007).

Sitting on top of these primitive and older regions of our subcortex lies our prefrontal cortex, which gets involved in managing the drives, lusts, love, and intimacy originating from the limbic region (Francesco and Cervone 2014; Zeki 2007). Interestingly, our experience of love restricts judgment of self or others, and it restricts unnecessary analysis or comparison, permitting the overwhelming positive feeling. This occurs because the prefrontal and cortical regions— including the temporal-parietal junction and the temporal horns critical to judgment, moral behavior, and awareness of self versus other—are deactivated, permitting the guilt-free flow of pleasure, romance, and love (see fig. 4).

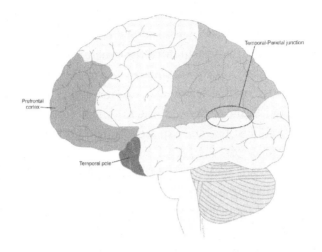

Figure 4. Judgment and morality centers of the brain

Indeed, it is often suggested that "they are head over heels in love" or "they are crazy in love." It is true that the frontal lobe deactivation essentially lets the beautiful flow of love emerge and take over our being without negative judgments or moral analysis (Zeki 2007). It is also true that such lack of judgment and moral compass when one feels blooming romance or love can indeed result in atypical behavior and perhaps lead to a red face or apology! When the reward system is hurt, such as with a breakup, the insula and these cortical regions of judgment get engaged, and neuroscience has taught us that the brain does not distinguish the pain from social rejection from that of physical injury! Such emotional pain then can lead to clinical depression and anxiety, and our brains end up out of balance. The good news, and the focus of this chapter, is that our brains have been granted the structure and chemistry to be *positive*, to *feel love and pleasure*, and to *share with others*.

The focus of this chapter is on our ability to express positive and healing energy-spirit to others. In order to do this, we first must feel and experience these positive feelings ourselves all across our cortex and deep inside our limbic reward center and make the conscious intention to share with others. In making a conscious intention to share our love, hope, joy, and forgiveness with others, we are engaging and triggering our prefrontal cortex (see fig. 3). This means that we not only rev up our reward system deep in our subcortex and related limbic system (see fig. 3); we consciously move from the feeling state to the action state and integrate the subcortex with the prefrontal cortex to bring healing to the world around us!

It is quite natural to want to share with those whom we love. However, the even more powerful sharing and healing within and without is when we share such love and positivity with those we do not know or where a strained relationship exists. This can actually be done every day regardless of what is done to us as we have been taught by Jesus to "forgive those who trespass against us" and by following his commandment "To love one another as you wish to be loved." While not easy, our expression of what I refer to as *spiritual medicine* can be healing, calming, and contagious—capable of diffusing tension and perhaps even of stopping wars! Our ability to give, to be generous, to forgive, and to love is also a most powerful medicine for ourselves with long-term benefits, unlike any derived pharmaceutical ones in existence.

Once again, all this power and ability to heal within, to bring peace and harmony to our inside, and to connect in a loving and healing way with others on the outside lie *within our brain, granted us by God.* His message for each of us to tap our spiritual power and to share with those who transgress against us and to the least among us was made crystal clear many years ago. His emphasis on love, forgiveness, faith, kindness, and humility necessitated his granting humans the hardware and ability to live a life filled with such healing powers. It is up to each of us to be open to his message and to work each day on engaging our internal Spirit to not only heal within but to help bring peace, harmony, and love to others.

It is important to spend time thinking about what powers, what healing chemistry, we might possess inside our being that we can tap and use to bring peace and harmony to our own organism. Likewise, we should consider how we could use these same spiritual powers to bring love, peace, and harmony to others in the world around us. This is particularly true where tension and angst exist, where the seeds of hatred have sown a wedge between family members and nations, and where vulnerability and loss of hope are pervasive.

Earlier we learned about the neural circuitry and neurochemistry critical to our positive feelings. Now I will turn again to scripture to help us identify and interpret what these healing powers or spiritual medicines are so that we can begin to share it with others. St. Paul offers some guidance on this matter in Galatians 5:13–26 (italics added):

> Out of *love*, place yourselves at one another's service. The whole law has found its fulfillment in this one saying: "*You shall love your neighbor as yourself.*" If you go on biting and tearing one another to pieces, take care! You will end up in mutual destruction! My point is that you should live in accord with the spirit and you will not yield to the cravings of the flesh.
>
> The flesh lusts against the spirit and the spirit against the flesh; the two are directly opposed. This is why you do not do what your will intends. If you are guided by the spirit, you are not under the law. It is obvious what proceeds from the flesh: lewd conduct, impurity, licentiousness, idolatry, sorcery, hostilities, bickering, jealousy, outbursts of rage, selfish rivalries, dissensions, factions, envy, drunkenness, orgies, and the like. I warn you, as I have warned you before: those who do such things will not inherit the kingdom of God!
>
> In contrast, the *fruit of the spirit* is *love*, *joy*, *peace*, *patient endurance*, *kindness*, *generosity*, *faith*, *mildness*, and *chastity*. Against such, there is no law!…Since we live in the spirit, let us follow the spirit's lead. Let us never be boastful, or challenging, or jealous, toward one another.

St. Paul (Corinthians 13:1–13) educates us further on our internal spiritual medicine that is most powerful and capable of healing unlike all other (italics added):

> Now I will show the way which surpasses all the others. If I speak with human tongues and angelic as well, but do not have love, I am a noisy gong, a clanging cymbal. If I have the gift of prophecy and, with full knowledge, comprehend all mysteries, if I have faith great enough to move mountains, but have not love, I am nothing. If I give everything I have to feed the poor and hand over my body to be burned, but have not love, I gain nothing.
>
> Love is patient; love is kind. Love is not jealous, it does not put on airs, it is not self-seeking, it is not prone to anger; neither does it brood over injuries. Love does not rejoice in what is wrong but rejoices with the truth. There is no limit to love's forbearance, to its trust, its hope, its power to endure.
>
> *Love never fails.* Prophecies will cease, tongues will be silent, knowledge will pass away. Our knowledge is imperfect and our prophesying is imperfect. When the perfect comes, the imperfect will pass away. When I was a child I used to talk like a child, reason like a child. When I became a man I put childish ways aside. Now we see indistinctly, as in a mirror; then we shall see face to face. My knowledge is imperfect now; then I shall know even as I am known. *There are in the end three things that last: faith, hope, and love, and the greatest of these is love.*

So what might these writings mean? What might we learn from them? This book is about our exploration into the purpose of the brain. I have proposed that the brain is a gift granted from God so that we may commune with God and live our lives according to his will. It follows then that our brain has also been granted certain capacities to affect or interact with our internal organism and to affect those around us, including other things and other forms of energy. In specific terms, this chapter provides those capacities, those ingredients originating within our brains that can be tapped, experienced, and shared to bring peace and healing within and to others. I refer to these as our own spiritual medicine; and Jesus, through St. Paul, has written the prescription for us. I discuss this prescription with my patients in my own practice, and I believe it is significantly underutilized in Western and perhaps all medicine today.

It is most likely not coincidental that the "Fruits of the Spirit" articulated above by St. Paul coincide quite well with our reward system in the brain and provide us with the spiritual and emotional health so necessary in our lives. The power, energy, and spiritual medicine lie within our brain, most likely within or related to the reward system (see fig. 3 and 4) and have become an increasingly popular topic of neuroscience and clinical practice.

I believe the searching I see in others, which really represents a rather desperate attempt to fill a void in one's life, can be stopped because the answers really lie within each of us, not in a bottle, artificial ingredient, procedure, or device. While not easy and certainly not quick, I encourage everyone to think deeply about the following *prescription for spiritual health* and all the healing it can provide you and others in your life. I will focus our prescription for spiritual health on six of the Fruits of the Spirit to include *love, forgiveness, faith, humility, kindness,* and *hope.*

Love

There is a very clear message communicated to us from the teachings of Jesus and the writings of St. Paul outlined above. *Love* is the single greatest spiritual medicine we humans possess, and it has the ability and power to heal everything else. This does not necessarily mean that pure love will cure a disease, but it does mean that concepts of cure, terminal, life and death may be viewed differently when one feels and expresses unconditional love and understands the salvation that is possible through love.

Interestingly, psychology and, more recently, neuroscience have studied the emotion or phenomenon of love (Francesco and Cervone 2014; Esch and Stefano 2005) advancing an understanding of the neuronal correlates of love. It is generally agreed that love is a complex neurobiological experience relying on trust, belief, pleasure, and the *reward center* within the brain, particularly the more primitive and older regions such as the limbic system (see fig. 2 and 3). This area of the brain evolved many years prior to the cortex. Limbic processes and our reward center involve oxytocin, vasopressin, dopamine, and serotonin signaling, which underlie the experience of love and those emotional factors listed above. What results is a pleasurable and rewarding experience that humans seek to reproduce and likely is necessary for survival of our species. The integration of the neurobiological aspects of love with the psychological and social can be useful to medicine and relate well to today's "integrative medicine" that studies the mind-body dynamic. It is true that the positive aspects of love do offer a stress-reducing, immune-enhancing, and health-promoting function that can lead to overall well-being.

I want to emphasize two factors with this brief overview of love and the brain. First, the region of the brain responsible for love is both primarily primitive and old, evolving many years prior to the more advanced cerebral cortex. Indeed, as we learned earlier, love involves deactivation of the more evolved prefrontal cortex, temporal-parietal junction, and temporal poles so that our experience of love is not jaded with judgment and negativity! Second, neuroscience underscores the health-promoting benefit of love and relates the experience of love to the brain. This fits, therefore, with the general premise of my book that our brains are granted health-promoting forces or spiritual energy, such as love, and that our expression of such promotes health. We simply have not prioritized our own healing powers with our brain, including love, to capitalize on improving our lives.

It really is not that easy to define *love*, though most, if not all, of us can relate to our own experience(s) in life when we felt love and when we expressed love. Sometimes love is expressed and shared with an animal, and sometimes it is felt with a memory of a loved one who has passed away. We can all probably describe the butterflies in our stomachs, the inner sense of euphoria, anticipation, and overall joy that love brings. There is certainly a "rush" when we find romance, when we obsess on the person we are falling in love with, and the overwhelming pleasure of uniting. We also can recall a time when we were careful to prepare a meal, an event, or select a gift that was done out of love and how good that felt knowing our gesture was to be received by someone we have strong, positive feelings for.

It is said that love conquers all, and St. Paul's writings support this idea as provided by Jesus. The overwhelming feeling of love with all its positive aspects and sense of unity seems to have the power to deflate any presence or hint of negativity or angst (remember, the judgment centers of our brain in the cortex are deactivated; see fig. 4). There is a type of unity with love, a bond formed between two or more that prevents divide or ill will. It is nearly impossible to have a toxic or negative feeling or state of mind when love is being expressed.

Love can lead to intimacy and indeed to the creation of another human. Sexual intercourse is the clearest example of two becoming one in a loving union. It is the rendering of complete vulnerability to another with trust and communion, as perhaps only God could intend. Even a hug, holding of hands, and an assertive *I love you* can be powerful and healing. How can such a feeling, a phenomenon, be health promoting, and why should love be practiced by everyone on a daily basis? Why should love be prescribed to all patients, regardless of condition?

Practice Love

It is not necessarily easy, though it is indeed natural, to express love. This is quite easily done with a baby or a puppy, though not so easy with one where we have a disagreement. It certainly is not shared with other teams, companies, nations that we do not get along with or that we view as enemies. Interestingly, Jesus instructed us to "love one another as ourselves." He did not instruct us to love only those who love us. In fact, we are to love regardless of response and regardless of what others think of us. That can be a difficult challenge even within the blood family, let alone another company or nation. It probably seems outlandish if we are asked to love someone who has physically injured, betrayed, lied, or otherwise neglected us. The more common and unfortunate response/emotion we use is anger. Unfortunately—and certainly countering the prescriptive power of love—anger and bitterness are the triggers for separation, division, and even war. So our task is to not only recognize the brilliant well-being that love has for our emotional and spiritual health but to also express and share our love, starting with those who we might think least deserve it.

A brain that is experiencing bitterness, anxiety, sadness, anger, irritability, impatience, hostility, isolation, or fear is out of balance. The prefrontal cortex and judgmental regions of the brain are likely too involved; and gossip, judgment, envy, and our comparison of self to others dominate (see fig. 4)! Our reward system is silent—no oxytocin, no dopamine, and no euphoria (no *ahhhhh*!). There is very little, if any, rhythm or harmony in such a brain. The rest of the body will follow the blueprint established by the brain, and as a result, the possibility of inflammation and a reduced immune system becomes real.

The same is true for anxiety and depression with social and emotional isolation, and even negative rumination. This leads to sleep disruption, irritability, irritable bowel syndrome, headache, hypertension, obesity, etc. Our typical treatment approach for this brain is to medicate with an antidepressant, antipsychotic, or antianxiety pill. There may also be a recommendation for psychotherapy, exercise, or perhaps meditation. It is very seldom that a clinician trained in Western medicine will even consider spirituality in the form of love as a treatment option. Given the fact that neuroscience suggests that love is an old, primitive, and entrenched function/feeling of the human brain, it seems reasonable to think that our organism might benefit from expression and practice of love since it sits at our core existence. If the practice of love can set in motion a cascade of the positive chemistry and physiology described above, then such an intervention makes perfect sense for all—but particularly, for a brain that has not experienced the positive consequences of love. (This is why I always teach medical students and nurses to defer to the "spiritual medicine cabinet" and to prescribe love, forgiveness, and kindness using their script pad!)

Neural plasticity facilitates the ability for a brain to change and not remain static. Unfortunately, the brain will develop what I call *defaults* over time, and sometimes these defaults (methods of thinking or behaving as a primary response) are not healthy. For example, one brain may react primarily with irritability or anxiety, and another with anger or depression. The brain develops these emotions as the default, and over time, it becomes difficult for the brain to change course to a new (novel and complex) response that is healthy. The practice of love is precisely the new (yes, complex) and healthy default response we want to develop for our personal health and for the health and well-being of others. It is possible, and Jesus taught us this path long ago. Engage the reward system (see fig. 3).

I would like all practicing clinicians on the planet, particularly those who have the courage, to *prescribe love* to all your patients for the remainder of your working lives. I also encourage all persons reading this book to practice love in your daily life using the following tips:

1. Start your day by consciously announcing to your brain or to another what you love in life. Do not take people or things for granted. This includes Jesus.

2. Tell a family member each day that you love him or her and hug them.

3. Tell your spouse or partner each day that you love him or her and hug them.

4. Tell all your children you love them each day and hug them extratight.

5. Pray to Jesus and God each day and express your love to him and smile.

6. Look to the sky, trees, mountains, water, and nature and express your love daily.

7. Make it a point each day to express love to someone with whom tension exists (not easy, but powerful for your spiritual and overall health) and smile.

8. Sit in quiet meditation and prayer and seek the path to being open to the healing power of love and to the opportunity and ability to share love with those around you, regardless of reciprocity.

9. Close your eyes and take three to five slow deep breaths and use your brain to remember an experience in your life filled with love. Pay attention to the warmth, calming sense, and pleasure you feel. What a medicine!

10. Commit to at least one loving statement to another each day. You can use any form of communication so long as it is expressed every day.

Forgiveness

> Father, forgive them for they do not know what they are doing. (Luke 23:34)

As difficult as it may be to "love one another as you wish to be loved," it is likely even more difficult to forgive, particularly when you perceive the emotional wound and insult from another to be deep. Forgiveness, however, is a critical and unwavering teaching from Jesus:

> Then Peter came up and asked him, "Lord, when my brother wrongs me, how often must I forgive him? Seven times?" "No," Jesus replied, "not seven times; I say, seventy times, seven times." (Matthew 18: 21–22)

> Because you are God's chosen ones, holy and beloved, clothe yourselves with heartfelt mercy, with kindness, humility, meekness, and patience. Bear with one another; forgive whatever grievances you have against one another. Forgive as the Lord has forgiven you. (Colossians 3:12–13)

> Get rid of all bitterness, all passion and anger, harsh words, slander and malice of every kind. In place of these, be kind to one another, compassionate and

mutually forgiving, just as God has forgiven you in Christ. (Ephesians 4:31–32)

Perhaps most poignant of all is Jesus's assertion that our own sins will be forgiven only when we forgive those who sin against us:

When you stand to pray, forgive anyone against whom you have a grievance so that your heavenly Father may in turn forgive you your faults. (Mark 11:25)

In her book *Neurotheology Reveals the Covert Bondage of Unforgiveness* (2009), Rosie M. Hill describes how anger and a lack of forgiveness relates to the brain's autonomic nervous system, which sets in motion our survival and fight-and-flight mode (remember the amygdala we discussed earlier?). She provides the blueprint for illness, reduced immune system function, and poor physical and mental health as our inability to forgive. Ms. Hill's book details specific scripture to help connect the spiritual dimension of forgiveness with brain function. She also proposes specific methods to help each of us forgive, let go, and free ourselves of all the negativity associated with being unforgiving. Much of what she teaches is built on the foundation of neural plasticity, which enables a change in our neurochemistry and feelings from a change in our thinking. Once again, our neural energy enables a change in our internal organism from a change in our mental thought!

One of the unfortunate truths of being human is that our natural default is to be negative and that we need to work to be positive. Interestingly, when I am in front of several hundred people, I will ask those who are positive to raise their hands. Nearly everyone in the audience raises their hands as expected. I then put them through an exercise that essentially taps their subconscious and ask them to say out loud something they see on the screen in front of them for a second. While their response need not be negative, nearly everyone across my audience responds with a negative message. Once they have a second to hear what they said, I then show the same information for longer than a second, permitting their cortex to get involved; and once the information becomes conscious, their perception of the content changes, and they respond with a positive statement.

My point with the exercise is to prove our subconscious, our default, is negative. We need to work to be positive, and by being conscious of our behavior and thoughts, we can be positive. Another quick example of this is when your child comes home with a report card and is proud to show you that he or she has earned three As and a C. Our focus tends to go directly to the C rather than affirming the hard work that must have gone into earning three As. Once again, being negative is our natural default, and we need to work at being positive.

Why is being negative our natural default? Many years ago, when we were roaming the planet with a primitive existence, we were under constant threat from large animals wishing us harm and, perhaps, even considering us as the next happy meal! This is how our amygdala evolved to have such an important role in our limbic system as it served as an alarm to our brain and body that our survival was in jeopardy.

During these moments of terror, our brains set in motion our autonomic nervous system, which interfaces with our endocrine system, causing our heart to beat fast, our pulse to race, our lungs to enlarge to accept the needed increased oxygen, our biceps and quads to receive increased blood as we are getting ready to run or to fight. As we learned earlier, our reward system is not activated, and all the pleasure chemicals are not flowing. We are hyperfocused on that which threatens us, and we do not have the ability to focus on any positive aspects of our internal being or of our environment. Our brains learned over time to develop the negative as our default, and as a result, we need to work to be positive!

Humans and Forgiveness

I personally believe that the ability to forgive purely and without exception is perhaps one of the most difficult behaviors for human beings. Part of the reason is because of our negative default set in stone in our DNA. We do have the ability to change our negative default, but it too is difficult. It is quite easy to form and to hold grudges, to gossip, to be judgmental, to compare self to others, to be negative toward others, and to be insulted sometimes even by nonthreatening communication and behavior. It is fair to say our society has only become more sensitive in our age of political correctness. Everyone has a cause, a grudge, and one can very easily become a victim and enter some form of antagonistic litigation. It is difficult to be positive.

What are the consequences of such feelings and thoughts? Recall that the message formed from a thought in the brain carries the blueprint for the rest of the body. You are the only living organism on the planet that can make yourself miserable or happy from a mere thought! What thought are you going to choose? From a negative thought, the brain delivers instructions to the amygdala, judgment centers of the cortex in the frontal, temporal, and parietal lobes; triggers norepinephrine and adrenaline in the brain and body; initiates our endocrine system to perfuse hormones such as cortisol and glucocorticoids into our blood stream, reaching our brain. This then causes our heart to beat and all the fight-and-flight responses described earlier.

Along the way, and particularly if this response becomes chronic, our brain and body begin to break down. Our cognition will be impaired. We will become irritable and risk mood disorder and anxiety. We may incur inflammation. Our immune system will suffer. Our bodies will react with head pain, stomach pain, back pain, irritable bowel syndrome, sleep disorder, nutritional deficits, and even ulcers. Our personal and occupational functioning will suffer, and we simply will not feel very good. In essence, our brains have lost their required balance and rhythm. Spiritually we are lost, and our lives are run by stress. The default has been set, and it is negative.

From such a context and reality that is the American culture, forgiveness is nearly impossible. We Americans are hurried, fatigued, digitally obsessed, and overwhelmed at least some part of the day, and that percentage of the day I just described is growing. This is why, in my opinion, there is such a frantic searching by many for the pill, cream, product, device, etc., to fix me! Once again, the searching can stop; for our neural energy, derived from a spiritual power granted to our brain, sits within us and does not cost anything. What is needed to engage this inner power is to become conscious of your behavior, to be aware of those triggers and stimuli that are causing the brain to lose balance. Forgiveness becomes an opportunity for each of us to not only become conscious but to engage this inner spiritual power to heal within and without.

Make an overt decision to be conscious of your thoughts, feelings, relationships, and how your brain and body react to each other. Next, permit yourself to let go of the negativity, grudges, and resentment, bitterness, and anger, if only for a small part of the day to begin. Visualize the reward system in your brain (see fig. 3) so that you can set in motion the spiritually therapeutic medicine of love, joy, kindness, compassion, pleasure, and peace, which will perfuse your brain and body. Forgiveness is a highly contagious path to get your reward system engaged, to calm the negative apparatus of your brain (tell your amygdala to calm down), and to bring immediate balance and spiritual harmony to your insides.

The good news is life itself brings us wonderful and nearly daily experiences for each of us to practice forgiveness. Sometimes it might be a small thing, like someone showing road rage at us or someone insulting us in front of others. It might be a more egregious act, such as being lied to, betrayed, or other breach of trust from a friend, lover, or family member. Perhaps most severe is becoming the victim of a crime against us or a family member. The bad news is that life provides a seemingly endless litany of acts of shame, betrayal, and unkindness that making such a list is not hard. From this reality of life, however, comes our opportunity to practice forgiveness.

Recall our exercise earlier when I asked you to sit quietly, take a deep breath, and to close your eyes? Please try this again.

Exercise 1: Open versus Closed

I would like you to stand tall in a relaxed position. Take a deep breath. Now open your arms to the side of your body with your palms facing up and be as open and wide as you can be. Pretend you are going to hug all your favorite people in life and open those arms so everyone can be included. Close your eyes and experience what this feels like. What are the feelings, sensations, and thoughts associated with this position? Before you open your eyes, I want you to *smile* and experience how your body reacts to the smile.

Now relax again, and this time, I want you to take both arms and hug yourself, tightly wrapping both arms around yourself without hurting yourself. If you want, bend over a bit and become closed off. Hold this position for fifteen seconds and pay close attention to how you feel and what emotions and thoughts you might experience in this position.

Now relax and again stand tall and open your arms real wide with palms facing upward to the sky as you stretch them out to your side. *Smile.* What are the feelings you experience? Are you able to distinguish the difference between a body position that permits openness and one that is closed off?

Are you open or closed in your own life?

Jesus and Forgiveness

A useful reminder to keep in your conscious brain is to visualize Jesus hanging on a cross, naked, yet forgiving those who killed him. How much humility, shame, despair, and courage must he have felt? This is a good reminder for us in our daily lives when we are feeling bitterness inside and when forgiveness is not in our hearts or brains! Can we not bring ourselves to forgive an act of another even if it is directly against us, particularly when we consider how Jesus forgave even in his dire circumstances of death? I often utter the words *naked on a cross* to help reorient my focus toward a healthy Spirit and a pure path.

Jesus was quite clear in his teachings that we need to be forgiving, without limit and regardless of the act against us, if we want to gain salvation. His clarity on this point, reinforced throughout scripture, leads any reasonable person to believe that forgiveness is important and needs to be practiced. It is fair to also state that forgiveness is not easy, and this is probably by design. Salvation and being like Jesus is not easy, nor is hanging naked on a cross!

I have many conversations with others about the complexity of forgiveness and how difficult it is to really forgive. Forgiveness is absolute and pure. There is no middle ground. You cannot forgive while stating, "I will never forget." Let the bitterness, anger, hostility, and vengeance leave your brain so that the rest of your body can balance. By not forgiving, you have reinforced your judgment and comparative centers where negativity lives (frontal lobes, parietal–temporal junction, temporal horns; see fig. 4). You have shut off your reward center (see fig. 3), where peace, pleasure, and positive energy reside. You have been blessed with the power to choose which path you wish to take, what brain center you want to trigger, and how you want your entire body to feel. It begins with a choice of thought and belief, and forgiveness is a direct route to your reward center and felling the *ahhhhh*!

I would like all practicing clinicians on the planet, particularly those who have the courage, to *prescribe forgiveness* to all your patients for the remainder of your working lives.

I also encourage all persons reading this book to practice forgiveness in your daily life using the following tips:

1. Visualize Jesus on the cross hanging naked and read or recall his words of forgiveness to those who killed him. Become conscious of forgiveness in your life.

2. Think about your own transgressions against others and ask for your own forgiveness. This is an important and necessary step to spiritual and overall health as it cleanses self from negativity and self-blame, bitterness, and hostility.

3. Think of others who have harmed or betrayed your trust and begin the process of letting go, forgiving, and forgetting. See the hostility leaving your body and understand that such forgiveness is about your health.

4. Speak openly to others about your quest to be forgiving as this will keep the journey conscious and focused.

5. Let others know directly that you have forgiven them for their behavior.

6. Engage in quiet moments daily of closing your eyes, connecting with your neural energy and spiritual self, and simply letting go of any negativity, gossip, and ill will.

7. Smile and live humbly and quietly with an intent for all verbal output to be positive and kind. Otherwise, remain silent until the negativity passes.

8. Recite the "Our Father" daily and focus on the part that teaches us to "forgive us our trespasses as we forgive those who trespass against us."

9. Be conscious on a daily basis of the opportunity for you to be forgiving and to refrain from the poisons of judgment and gossip. This is the path to internalized and expressed anger and a brain out of balance.

10. Experience the lift, the release, of emotional and toxic weight from your brain and body. It is important to rejoice in the positive and healthy feelings of forgiveness and the emptying of the negativity that is damaging your health.

Checking In with You

Part of the journey toward spiritual and neural health is our need to be conscious of our internal being. Are you in balance and in harmony with the energies of others and the universe? Are you at peace with God and free of guilt, anger, sadness, or bitterness? These are important matters that most do not understand or attend to. We cannot achieve neurospiritual health and the changes necessary to accomplish such if we are not first conscious of where we are internally. As I have asserted throughout this text, we all have neural energies granted us by God in the form of spiritual energy, which we can use to heal within, to achieve balance and harmony, and to unite without. The first step is to check in with yourself and conduct a spiritual and emotional scan of your brain and body.

Try to do this now by closing your eyes and becoming overtly conscious of how you feel and what troubles, if any, you are experiencing. What are the sources of these ill feelings, and how intense are they? Do you believe you can rid yourself of these toxins, and are you willing to engage the spiritual medicine of love, forgiveness, faith, humility, kindness, and hope necessary to free yourself of such toxins? Critical to this is your understanding that the Fruits of the Spirit have been granted to you and lie within your brain to provide you the path to real health. It is now up to each one of us to tap this gift of spiritual healing.

At this point, what is your experience of love and forgiveness? These are two prominent medicines we control and, if properly realized and engaged, will bring us unity and peace. Can you stop and turn inward and assess your own levels of love and forgiveness? Try to feel love and be willing to share with others as forgiveness will flow naturally from love. Similarly, if you are willing to forgive those who have harmed you, your brain and body will experience love and a sense of unity with the energy around you. You are in control of this opportunity, and best of all, there are no side effects or contraindications! What does the gauge of your love and forgiveness say, empty or filled? Time to fill her up and share it with others.

Faith

Now faith is the substance of things hoped for, the evidence of things not seen. (Hebrews 11:1)

Faith is a tough one for humans because it involves risk and a commitment to something we do not see or completely understand. I sometimes wonder if there are even similar earthbound behaviors of faith that we engage in. Do we know where our wife or husband is when she or he leaves the home in the morning? We do not, yet we continue to love our spouse because we have faith in them. The only thing the binds the relationship and the commitment is faith, sometimes referred to as blind love or blind faith. Perhaps we have a best friend who we know will be there for us if something goes wrong and we need them. While such a premise is purely hypothetical, we nonetheless have a firm belief that our friend would be by our side in time of need. Once again, this is pure faith! When faith is broken, we are hurt emotionally and feel a sense of betrayal. We get fooled and experience shock because faith is indeed without defense or suspicion—it is pure. These are but two earthbound examples of how faith plays in our lives and how we live by faith in ourselves and in others.

For some, faith in God seems to mandate another level of scrutiny and doubt. This is not new since even one of the disciples of Jesus did not have faith. This is true despite the fact that Thomas saw the acts of Jesus and heard the word of Jesus directly in his presence.

> Thomas, because you have seen Me, you have believed. Blessed are those who have not seen and yet have believed. (John 20:29)

Hence the phase *doubting Thomas*, which has become part of our lexicon in society. We need to see and to touch to be sure, but faith is born not from what is seen and touched but rather what is not seen and not touched. Do you believe in God, and why do you believe in God? This is an important question because it forces you to explore your own belief system and your spirituality. That is a wonderful thing for all of us to do. As I stated earlier in this book, I am a follower of Jesus Christ, but I am not an expert in my own religion. I can state unequivocally, however, that I have infinite faith in Jesus Christ as my Savior and as the Son of God who came to this earth to save us from our sins. I believe he is with me at all times, and I believe I have the ability to lead my life as Christ wants me to.

The key word there is *ability* as I certainly fall short (sin) and need to seek forgiveness for my shortcomings. Consider your own thoughts and feelings about your own faith and belief system. Your spirituality is a foundational part of you that is perhaps most important for your overall health and well-being. Our spiritual health is a lifelong journey, and there can be turns and twists in our path as we are subjected to tests of our faith. The strength of our faith is certainly tested in hard times, with loss and with grief. The path can be difficult, similar to hanging naked on a tree, but it is at these times in our life that we learn not only about ourselves but also about our spiritual strength and whether our faith can help us overcome.

In my own practice, I hear many stories of human peril and how faith has either triumphed or has been rejected. The patient commonly feels anger and bitterness toward God, and there is a type of spiritual divorce that has occurred. I believe it is important to help the patient work through these feelings as I know he or she once had a terrific relationship with God and that their spiritual life was a cornerstone or at least a strong part of their identity. The loss of a significant other (human or God) leaves our identity fragmented and unhealthy. We feel lost, and this leads directly to the searching behavior I described earlier.

So often, the void is filled with toxic emotions, unhealthy and illegal substances, and poor judgment. We are prone to hide from our realities, using unhealthy masks that never really solve the problem. I have learned over many years that humans can become whole again and that the spiritual dimension of our identity is often the primary path to healing. I was not taught this in all my years of education, and I arrived at this belief only after many interactions with people in significant distress and hopelessness. One of the critical parts of their identity—and indeed, for some, their primary source of healing—was temporarily divorced as they shielded themselves from their faith. By turning back to their faith, especially during the most difficult times, they became whole again with their identity realized.

This is not to say that all other forms of treatment and healing are useless. I come from a traditional clinical, scientific background, and my personal belief is that we are not that advanced in the medical field to believe a big toolbox is not needed! Recall the past twenty or more years I have been teaching the general public about the power of a holistic Brain Health Lifestyle®. By holistic, I mean meeting the person or patient where he or she is, and sometimes that means having a prescription for spiritual healing ready in the toolbox.

The last thing we need is a rigid, defensive, and restrictive care system. That is not holistic but rather egocentric, formed from the needs or beliefs of the provider and not the person seeking healing. My hope with this approach is to expand the healing professions in the United States to use our intelligence and positions of healing to better understand what patients are asking for. It tends not to be medical in nature, and the belief system is critical to fortify from the provider to the patient. Attitude matters; will to live matters; and so does love, forgiveness, and indeed, faith! Take out the prescription pad and have the courage to jot down the word *faith* on it and hand it to your patient. Can you imagine adding curriculum to the medical and related health-care education in the

United States that pertains to what I am referring to in this text as *neurospiritual healing*?

I have found personally a great advantage and benefit from having such a strong faith, conviction, and commitment to Jesus. It removes doubt from my brain and, hence, from my body. I have worked to generate a strong spiritual foundation for my life, and this has placed ease in and around me. Earthbound matters are less heavy, less overwhelming, and less of a priority. My faith has helped me truly believe "it is okay," and the *it* means everything. There are greater matters of priority than what exists in tangible and material things. Health always trumps wealth, and family is necessary. The chemistry that defines our healing, unity, and ease with earthbound matters originate from the Fruits of the Spirit, to include love, forgiveness, faith, humility, kindness, and hope.

Our brains were granted these potent healing chemicals, and they are ready for us to feel them, apply them, and to heal using them not only within but with those who are in need. You have a wonderful opportunity to be freed from the shackles of earthbound problems, both small and large, though all seem large. Be free and experience the spiritual harmony and balance that is granted you within your brain and will flow throughout your body to literally influence those around you. This is the path of neurospiritual healing, and it is provided to us from God via our brain for use at any time.

I would like all practicing clinicians on the planet, particularly those have the courage, to *prescribe faith* to all your patients for the remainder of your working lives. I also encourage all persons reading this book to practice faith in your daily life using the following tips:

1. Stop and take some time to be conscious and assess your own faith from a historical, current, and future perspective. Where have you been? Where are you now? And where would you like your faith level to be in the future?
2. Has your faith changed in your life? How?
3. What are the circumstances or factors that changed your faith?
4. Define the positive attributes of having faith for your life and faith in God, yourself, and others?
5. Teach someone, particularly a younger person, the importance of faith and how it can be healing and empowering.
6. Feel the power of your faith when earthbound matters invade your brain and seduce you into obsessing about small things like materialism.
7. Say a daily prayer of thanks for your faith and ask for continued guidance to remain faithful.
8. Share the power of your own faith with others, particularly those who have no faith or have lost faith. Your spiritual energy can be healing to others.
9. Be open to the power of your faith and do not be afraid to express your needs.

10. Remain conscious about the power of your faith and keep it close to you as a primary tool to bring ease to a tense situation, solution to a problem, and healing to those in need.

Humility

Let nothing be done through selfish ambition or conceit, but in lowliness of mind let each esteem others better than himself. (Philippians 2:3)

God resists the proud, but gives grace to the humble. Humility cures worldliness. (James 4:6)

Humility involves a separation or divorce of self that must first be established within our cortex, the conscious part of our brain. We have to firmly set as a default our identity as one that is humble and not a random or coincidental act that surfaces episodically. In no small way, we must be willful in our pursuit of humility, and we must persist in our humble acts. It is through such repetition of thought and action that a neurological default will occur at the cellular level in our brain. In basic terms, our brain will know to be humble as that is who we are.

I wonder sometimes how hard it is to be humble in the United States as we tend to be a materialistic people. So often, our goals may be quite selfish with outcomes or success measured in terms of number, size, salary, square feet, etc. We are a competitive society, and while that is not necessarily bad, it seems winning may be misplaced alongside humility. When the currents of behavior are strong and heading in the competitive and materialistic direction, it can be hard indeed to not run with the herd. It takes strong conviction, confidence, and yes, faith to be humble. Perhaps humility is not so difficult if we place our success in places that are not earth bound. Maybe Spiritual health and unity with God is one way to divorce from our self and to turn our presence and future to His will, not ours.

The greatest example of humility is once again provided us by the story and image of Christ dying naked on the cross. The intent of crucifixion was not only physical pain but also open shame for the public to witness. Stripped of clothing and nailed to a tree is complete humiliation. Nonetheless, Jesus did so for all to forgive our sins, and he even forgave those who hurt him. The idea of shame is not conveyed from the story of the crucifixion. Indeed, Jesus's behavior turned shame on those who tortured and mocked him. It is a wonderful example of how to behave even when life is being lost and all earthly control is surrendered.

Perhaps even more illustrative of Jesus's humility is the fact that he was born in a manger set among farm animals. He reportedly was the son of a carpenter and worked himself as a carpenter at least for some period of time. His dress and appearance from all reports were quite modest, and his teachings were consistently about the power of humility and the unnecessary burdens of possessions and earthbound materials. He was not judgmental and, in fact, angered some for talking, eating, and staying with groups of people whom others frowned upon. He taught that the least among us are the chosen and that the last shall be first. This all adds to a presence and life on earth characterized as humble and modest. His behavior was to serve as a model not only in what he said to do but also, indeed, in how he lived his life.

We are surrounded each day with good people who behave in bad ways. Gossip remains a sin, and far too many will bring others down in order to appear more favorable for self. We are so quick to personalize, to be offended, and to attack others for what really is a simple difference of opinion. Politics is no longer a healthy debate of solutions and ideas to our social problems; it is divisive, personal, and insulting. We are fifty states that do not seem to be united and rather are divided in so many ways—from political party to income, skin color, religion, sexual orientation, etc. Somewhere along the way, the wrong message got communicated, and we forgot we are all the same and that, while differences can be a good thing, we are bound by far more commonality as a human with a brain and spiritual existence.

There is no doubt that the prescription for neurospiritual healing I am detailing in this book—to include love, forgiveness, faith, humility, kindness, and hope—can bring healing to the individual and to the nation. Indeed, such chemistry not only can unite the United States but the world all around us. The reason is that we are all human on this planet, and the vast majority of us will respond favorably to love, forgiveness, faith, humility, kindness, and hope. The fact that these Fruits of the Spirit have a positive impact and influence over humans—regardless of culture, geography, or age—illustrates how foundational they are to the human race. They are essential and natural to our DNA and are present in the very old parts of our brain.

I fear we do not completely understand the power of our spiritual being and how our daily expression and internalization of these Fruits can heal the individual, society, and the world. In this sense, healing is not about removal of disease but rather generating prioritization of our existence, bringing peace and balance to our inside and a unified communion all around us. I believe this is possible, but humility is certainly necessary as it removes selfishness and places others first.

I would like all practicing clinicians on the planet, particularly those who have the courage, to *prescribe humility* to all your patients for the remainder of your working lives. I also encourage all persons reading this book to practice humility in your daily life using the following tips:

1. Become conscious of your own selfishness and make an assessment of your own valuation of material things. Be honest so you know where you stand.

2. Begin the process of literally giving things away. Remove clothes, sporting gear, food, etc., from your

home to give to others in need. Such flushing of things is quite therapeutic.

3. Consider purchase of more humble goods that can produce the same outcome as those that might be purchased for selfish reasons or bravado.

4. Ask about others without offering anything of self unless asked.

5. Sit last at any board meeting or dinner gathering.

6. Introduce yourself as father, mother, or son or daughter and not your job title.

7. Refrain from gossip and walk away from conversations with gossip.

8. Refrain from putting others down and work on solutions.

9. Worry less about winning and more about preparation, hard work, and honesty. Win and lose well.

10. Spend time with others in need and be with those who have done wrong or who are vulnerable.

Kindness

But I say to you, love your enemies, bless those who curse you, do good to those who hate you, and pray for those who spitefully use you and persecute you, that you may be sons of your Father in heaven; for He makes his sun rise on the evil and on the good, and sends rain on the just and the unjust. (Matthew 5:44–45)

> Jesus said to him, "You shall love the Lord your God with all your Heart, with all your soul, and with all your mind. This is the first and great commandment. And the second is like it: You shall love your neighbor as yourself." (Matthew 22:37–39)

> Beloved, let us love one another, for love is God and everyone who loves is born of God and knows God. (John 4:7)

Kindness is a virtue that is built on one's concern for others. Kindness does imply action and a selfless way of life. We can always look to the life of Jesus to understand what kindness is and what it looks like. Scripture describes many stories in which Jesus helped those in need, those who were most vulnerable, and those who were without. Indeed, his message to "turn the other cheek, and to offer your coat if another piece of clothing is taken from you" also underscores the need to be kind to all, not just in cases where it is easy to be kind.

My wife and I attended an outdoor sunset mass in Aruba 2015, and since we did not have a rental car, we used a taxi to travel some distance to the Lady of Alta Vista Church that sits high on a hill and overlooks the Caribbean Sea while set among the desert that is Aruba (see photos in Appendix 2). The mass was beautiful, and when it was time to leave, we were hoping to find a taxi. Unfortunately, though not unexpectedly at this hour, there was no taxi. I realized I was going to need to ask a member of the church to call a taxi for my wife and me. I was not sure whom to ask, though something directed me to a young woman who was heading to her car with her male companion, perhaps her husband.

When I asked if she would be kind enough to call a taxi for my wife and me, she and her mother-in-law, who was with them, asserted that they would drive my wife and me to our hotel some distance from the church. It turns out that the husband of the older woman used to drive tourists around the island, and they felt committed to his legacy to offer us the kindness of a ride home. This is a wonderful example of unconditional kindness from complete strangers who are filled with the Fruits of the Spirit to act in a kind way, much to the benefit of my wife and me. Thank you to our friends in Aruba, and we hope to spread the same kindness to others in our lives.

Kindness certainly involves love and forgiveness, two other spiritual medicines I reviewed in this book. Like forgiveness, kindness can be very difficult for us when we feel another party does not deserve the empathy, compassion, and giving so inherent to kindness. However, Jesus taught us that kindness is unconditional and that we are to treat others as we wish to be treated. Sounds easy, but it is not. Too often, we are quick to anger, bitterness, and revenge. Consider our society today and ask how easy it would be for any of us to be kind to those who attack us, harm us, or slander us. This is true for international affairs and also for interpersonal matters between colleagues, companies, families, and even lovers!

Kindness seems not to be our default today. Rather, we lash out easily and wish harm on others, a direct refutation of Jesus's commandment. Personal attack is the norm, bullying is a common feature of childhood, and gossip is as rampant as ever. We can also neglect, ignore, and not respond to those we love, causing a type of "silent hostility." Our lack of kindness harms us first by shutting off our reward system and engaging our judgmental and comparative systems of the brain (see fig. 4).

As we learned earlier, the release of adrenaline, cortisol, and norepinephrine can be damaging to our brain and body. Road rage, hate crimes, domestic violence, fighting, yelling, rejection, silence, and insult are all forms of toxic emotional energy. This is not how Jesus taught us to live either by his teachings or by his behavior. We want to have as a goal each day to engage and trigger our reward system (see fig. 3), where our brains and bodies are bathed in positive emotional energy built from the spiritual presence granted us simply for being human. It is up to us to tap this spiritual medicine, and we can do it daily through intentional and random acts of kindness.

I encourage each of you to initiate an intentional or random act of kindness daily and be conscious of how you feel when you behave with such kindness. Regardless of the recipient's response to your kindness, how do you feel? I will suggest that if you are conscious of your feelings and emotional/spiritual being when you are kind, you will experience the free flow of positive emotional energy that is spiritually cleansing and healing. The reason is you are acting as Jesus acts, and your brain is uniting with a godly presence that bathes your brain and body with euphoria and warmth. This is the exact opposite reaction and feeling to acts of bitterness and revenge (amygdala gone wild!). The former is what Jesus taught and engages the reward system of the brain (see fig. 3) while the latter is opposite of what Jesus taught and engages the judgmental part of the brain (see fig. 4).

Acts of kindness are not difficult and do not need to involve money, expensive gifts, extensive time, grandiosity, publicity, or anything elaborate. I try to send a kind text to someone each day, and I try to fill my twitter @brainhealthctr with positive images and words. I do believe *words represent the single most activating neurochemical agent* we have! Words have the power to be long-lasting, to spark the reward system, and to remain deep within the folds and flaps of the conscious cortex. Jesus taught us that his words were the Spirit, and as noted earlier in this book, his words represented an early example of neural plasticity that continue to shape the brains of humans all across the planet, thousands of years after he walked the planet!

The first President Bush is famous for his written notes of support, which he sent to many people in his life circle and those he did not know. His words reportedly offered support and encouragement that we all can use in our daily lives. One of the great things about our digital world is our ability to affect so many people across the planet in a positive way simply by reaching out with our words. I am blessed to be in a position where I correspond almost daily with complete strangers in need all across the planet, and I offer words of support and hope so their day may be a little brighter. I also offer all my audiences the opportunity to contact me should they need to do so. I am not your doctor, but I can be a resource for information and a well of positivity and optimism when needed. I believe this is something I am obligated to offer as someone trying to be kind and to mimic the life of Jesus.

As noted above, acts of kindness can be easy and, at the same time, very difficult. The easy acts of kindness simply require us to behave, to engage, and to express our compassion and giving of self to others. This really is easy, though one wonders why we have a world where acts of kindness seem rare. Easy acts of kindness also tend to occur more frequently because the recipient of our kindness has not offended or harmed us. It is when we are harmed that acts of kindness become difficult, if not impossible. Similar to our inability to forgive, really and genuinely forgive, it is human nature to struggle and resist kindness to those who hurt us.

I watch the news on a daily basis, and it is truly sad how hate has filled our world. We see crimes of murder, rape, assault, robbery, and others occurring in our nation all too frequently. There is a loss of the respect for life so foundational to the formation of our country that is based on the Judeo-Christian doctrine taught us by Jesus. When a nation loses respect for life at any age, it begins to become insensitive to the horror of crime or unnecessary death. Such a nation loses its soul and identity and becomes malice to our greatest gift that is life. That gift is from God, and by ignoring this gift, we ignore God.

We see the ripple effects of such a disrespect for life in our television and movie industry, where violence is so common; in our digital entertainment world, with violent video games often the most popular; and in our political landscape, where we do not hear or see enough discussion on the importance of compassion, love, and respect for all life. Recall that the brain has plasticity that enables it to be shaped by the ongoing violence, crime, and loss of respect for life. This results in a nation filled with brains that have become insensitive to the beauty of life, to the teachings of Jesus, and to the importance of kindness to our fellow people.

I always pause when I hear the victim of a horrific crime offer forgiveness to the perpetrator. Perhaps a family member was attacked, raped, or murdered, and the spouse or relative of the victim will say that he or she will not give the criminal any power from unforgiveness. Indeed, I have seen people forgive publicly a criminal who has murdered their family member! This is remarkable to me because I know I would have a very hard time displaying the same Jesus-like behavior. My own tendency would probably be toward the judgmental and anger default, ignoring what I know to be the proper Jesus-like response. This tells me I have work to do on my own maturation and journey as a follower of Christ. This is where the act of kindness gets tough because the kindness is offered to someone who have hurt us in some way.

Acts of harm, violence, and death have always been present in society and represent a reality of being human. It is senseless behavior with no good outcome, but humans hurt and kill other humans. This is indeed upsetting, for we should know better. However, when we are in a society and world that is bombarded daily by examples of the lack of respect for life, we end up hurting one another, sometimes with little, if any, regard! This was true in all parts of world history and indeed continues to display its ugliness in the United Stated almost daily. I am quite clear that evil exists and that no acts of kindness will change some brains away from such evil.

I am also clear that there are times when a nation must do what is necessary to protect its people against such evil. War has been a reality of humankind since before Jesus's time, and it continues today in the most unfortunate ways. However, I do wonder if we have the ability to be kind to those who hurt us and if such acts of kindness over time can overcome the criminal, terror-filled, and hate-laced acts so common in our world today? Conversely, perhaps we can unite enough of the world around the spiritual medicine I have articulated and as taught many years ago by Jesus to overcome the minority of humans who reject such kindness and spiritual healing. Jesus's teachings tell us that kindness, love, and forgiveness are critical, as is hope, and that we must not turn our backs on these spiritual medicines as they are the path to real healing and unity.

To begin, acts of kindness require a conscious effort, same as the other spiritual medicines demand. We need to take a review of our own behavior, motivation, and desire to be kind to self and others. From the personal, we can then work toward kindness on a grander scale, where such acts are to serve as a unifying force for many around the world who do respect life and the goodness of humanity. It is true that we sometimes live in situations where such goodness is buried by force or brutal dictatorship, but the goodness is still there, waiting to bloom and get expressed.

I would like all practicing clinicians on the planet, particularly those who have the courage, to *prescribe kindness* to all your patients for the remainder of your working lives. I also encourage all persons reading this book to practice kindness in your daily life using the following practical tips:

1. Take some time to be conscious of your own level of kindness and review whether or not you have expressed kindness to your self or others recently.

2. Make a conscious decision to become kinder and to engage in acts that reflect kindness on a daily basis.

3. Do something kind for yourself to experience both the reward of giving and receiving kindness. It can be something small but meaningful to you.

4. Write a daily text, tweet, or Facebook post that offers kindness to someone specific or to society in general.

5. Give something away to the less fortunate. This can be extra food, clothing, or other resource.

6. Attempt to be kind to someone who has not been kind to you. Do so regardless of the person's response to you. Your act of kindness is for you.

7. Reach out to someone in need, even if the person is a stranger.

8. Do not be afraid to be more generous than you are.

9. Offer a daily prayer of kindness to others.

10. Call someone today and tell them how great they are or describe something about them that is great.

Hope

For whatever things were written before were written for our learning that we through the patience and comfort of the Scriptures might have hope. (Romans 15:4)

For I know the thoughts that I think toward you, says the Lord, thoughts of peace and not of evil, to give you a future and a hope. (Jeremiah 29:11–13)

Hope is such an important virtue to have for each of us. We need to have some belief that our lives have meaning, that there is a future filled with a positive outlook, and that no matter how difficult things may seem, we maintain this hope to guide us and help us persevere. Hope has been documented to be a primary reason why people confronted with enormous horror and pending death not only survived but were ultimately responsible for helping others in the same circumstance to also survive. Hope is a dynamic energy that can guide each of us in difficult moments when our health fails, finances erode, relationships end, and loss occurs. Hope is contagious and can be practiced. It is a part of a positive attitude and occurs when one focuses on the positive and refuses to be paralyzed by the negative. Because of plasticity, a daily exercise of positive thinking will stimulate neuronal (cellular) activation in your left frontal lobe, and over time, this region will become robust. More importantly, your default will become positive!

Hope can easily be lost when we experience difficulty and lose sight of our own resilience. It is during these times that a belief system in a higher power becomes critical. Consider this thought from St. Paul:

> Be anxious for nothing, but in everything by prayer and supplication, with thanksgiving, let your requests be made known to God: and the peace of God, which surpasses all understanding will guard your hearts and minds through Christ Jesus. (Philippians 4:6–7)

By remaining conscious of our own neural energy and the spiritual presence granted us from God, we can enjoy a sense of peace without anxiety or worry. As revealed earlier in this book, so many people live with feelings of anxiety, worry, and depression. There is great unease for so many, and this is what leads to the searching behavior as folks become somewhat desperate to find validation or security with self. Our spiritual being needs to be nurtured for such moments so that we never feel alone and so we always have an open dialogue with God, who wants us to speak to him through prayer. This is the definition of *hope* as it is always present and always results in spiritual healing no matter what occurs in our earthbound lives.

Hope is also something that can be shared and granted to others if we are genuinely hopeful ourselves. A positive attitude and optimistic energy is indeed contagious. Our hopefulness can be comforting to others who may be lost and without direction. So many people, particularly young people, make bad mistakes because they lack hope; they see only darkness and no light. Interestingly, *light* is the word used in the Bible so frequently in connection with God and the Holy Spirit. Light is considered hope—and love, a manifestation of God—and it represents the spiritual path for everyone to follow.

Hope can be generated from a strong spiritual presence in oneself and an understanding and belief that you are not alone. Hope, being something that is indeed contagious and therapeutic, needs to be communicated and exhibited by anyone with a position of influence. This means leaders of nations, doctors and nurses, teachers, coaches, and certainly parents and family members. We all can be more hopeful, more positive, and more optimistic. Once again, hope is easy when things are going well, but hope is not so easy when life takes a traumatic or devastating turn. I encourage everyone to maintain that image of Jesus hanging naked on a tree as he never lost hope, for He knew His Father was with Him and that His future was bright. The same can be true for each of us.

Indeed, it can be hard to follow a path of hope when we are barraged daily with images of death, horror, and terror. The evil in the world does exist, and it wants to control you and me. In our own daily lives, we are tempted and seduced to follow evil. By daily meditation, prayer, and the exercise of positive thinking, we can not only combat evil but defeat it! Hope, kindness, forgiveness, and the other Fruits of the Spirit are not easy, and I really do not think they are supposed to be easy. Something as powerful and as rewarding as living a life filled with such Fruits is meant to be difficult. We are being challenged in our conviction and desire to truly follow Jesus in His way.

As he stated many years ago, "I am the way." He did not say, "Act similar to me." He said, "I am the way." There does not seem to be too much wiggle room here. I can recall an older priest one time slowly walking to the microphone and bellowing out the idea that "they are not ten suggestions"! This brought clarity to me regarding my own life and our tendency to rationalize away behavior when that is not "the way."

So we all have moments in our lives when hope seems far away and darkness fills our day. That is being human, and it truly is difficult. However, try to view such experiences as an opportunity to show your conviction to remain positive, to maintain hope, and to understand that you are not alone in your spiritual journey.

I would like all practicing clinicians on the planet, particularly those who have the courage, to *prescribe hope* to all your patients for the remainder of your working lives. I also encourage all persons reading this book to practice hope in your daily life using the following practical tips:

1. Be conscious of your view of hope and how hopeful you are. Do you need to increase your level of hope?
2. Practice positive thinking on a daily basis so that you build the left frontal region of your cortex, which can lead to a default of positivity and hope.
3. List several reasons to be hopeful in your life. This might include people or things.
4. Think about the times of despair in your life and consider whether you were hopeful or not.
5. Do you think other people would describe you as hopeful?
6. Is there someone in your life whom you consider hopeful, and can you mimic this person?
7. Make it a conscious goal to become more hopeful, to remain convicted to a positive outlook no matter what life brings you.

8. List a few items you hope for at this time in your life. Begin a conscious effort to visualize them and to see these hopeful things as reality.

9. Speak to God daily about your hopes for yourself and for others.

10. Pray daily that hope may fill the lives of those who have lost hope so they can experience life and spiritual healing.

10

Putting It All Together

As in the summer of 2015, when I began writing this book, sitting across a panoramic view of the Atlantic Ocean (see Appendix 2), I find myself now in early December of the same year, sitting at a window of a high-rise hotel, looking out at the Caribbean Sea (see Appendix 2). The majesty and beauty are breathtaking. Earlier this morning, just prior to my writing the final chapter of this book, I was in the water, seemingly alone. The sun was hitting the beautiful water, making it look turquoise; and for some reason, I decided to look down as I walked the floor of the shallow sea. There, staring at me, was a large starfish as if saying hello and reminding me, "If we are open, nature will come and interact with us" (see Appendix 2). The evenings I spent on this island provided me a window into the complexity of nature at night simply by gazing at the hundreds of thousands of stars. How and why this occurs are the questions running through my brain. Random? I think not. So as I did in July of 2015, I again wondered about the miracle of my brain and its purpose. Random? I think not.

Grand Purpose of My Brain

I have proposed a grander purpose to my brain, to the human brain. This miraculous system that enables our identity, our sense of time, personality, emotions, cognitive ability, and motor skill is so complex we do not understand how it works. If we learn one day that the brain is in our head to conduct these functions and nothing else, we can all continue to marvel at the brain. However, I have written this book to assert that this is not the only purpose of our brain, for that would minimize its complexity. Our brain has a grander purpose that begins with the idea that God granted us a brain to ultimately communicate with him.

Jesus's teachings, as presented in the Bible, teach all to love, forgive, share, give, treat others as you would be treated, hear, see, taste, touch, and have faith. The brain is clearly necessary to process these teachings of Jesus, to have the ability to believe or not, and to lead a life that mimics Jesus in the hopes of gaining salvation. Indeed, the brain is the only system in the human body that permits the following of Jesus and even the refutation of Jesus and of God. It is from such a dichotomous reality that faith is born and bred. I completely understand the argument that God can create any vehicle or conduit for humans to communicate and interface with him. However, we have a brain, and it is the system in our bodies that permits us to choose to follow the teachings of Christ.

The brain being granted us by God, however, has other abilities within this grand purpose, including our ability to tap our spiritual power, which I refer to as *neural energy*, so we can help to bring balance and healing to ourselves. Similarly, our brains using the same spiritual power/neural energy have the ability to affect others in our environment. We can even use our God-given neural energy to interface with other energies that exist in nature. As I described in this book, if we can be open, nature will provide us many wonderful insights and experiences, such as the one I described above with my starfish and even me knowing whom to ask for a ride home after mass.

So the grand purpose of my brain is to communicate with God, to follow the life of Jesus, to use my internal Spirit and neural energy to heal within, to help my neighbor heal and find peace, and to remain open to the powerful energies that exist in our universe. Recognizing the similarities between the universe and brain, we can appreciate that both are vast and not understood, both are powerful, both require balance and rhythm, and both are tremendous energy sources that are yet untapped. Finally, the brain does interact with the universe all the time; and when we are open, we become conscious of the magic and reward such interaction produces.

The Brain and Spiritual Healing

The brain has a wonderful reward system (see fig. 3) that sits within an older (limbic) part of the brain and manages our sense of euphoria, joy, love, kindness, and positive energy. I call this our *ahhhhh* moments of life, and you know when your reward system is triggered! For some famous athletes like Michael Jordan, Tom Brady, Tiger Woods, and Roberto Clemente, the reward system manifests as "being in the zone." It is a pure sense of ease and joy, triumph and bliss, that feels as though life is carrying a performance along. Fortunately, all of us can be in the *zone*, as I was this morning when I saw my starfish. My reward system lit up!

It is true that the many structures of this reward system do respond to unnatural and potentially dangerous agents such as cocaine, pornography, and gambling. We call these dangers addictions, and it is the brain's reward system that becomes controlled by these substances and behaviors to create an unnatural sense of euphoria. Interestingly, our medical system utilizes faith (twelve-step program) as a primary means of breaking the addictive cycle! For purposes of this book, we are most interested in natural and safe agents such as those outlined in my prescription for spiritual healing originally authored by St. Paul's Fruits of the Spirit.

The structures of the reward system (see fig. 3) interact with one another and help to unleash a potent neurochemical (dopamine) that results in our feeling pleasure and joy. The hypothalamus sends oxytocin and vasopressin to the pituitary gland, which then releases both into the bloodstream, and we have our *ahhhhh* moment. The resulting feeling of overwhelming euphoria, bliss, happiness, peace, pleasure, and joy is possible for all of us at all times. We simply need to stimulate our reward system using proper and healthy behaviors and thoughts.

Interestingly, the reward system knows that judgment and moral comparisons are not helpful to feelings of euphoria. That is why an increase in dopamine reduces the presence of serotonin, and this leads to reduced activation of the frontal lobes, parietal-temporal junction, and even the temporal poles (see fig. 4), where judgment and morality-based analysis occurs. Pure bliss tends not to be the friend of guilt, judgment, or self-analysis, and thank goodness the brain figured this out!

More support for a grand purpose of the brain, God not only granted us a brain to communicate with him and to enable us to follow the path of Jesus, He provided the brain with a reward system so we could know euphoria and bliss. The teachings of Jesus as presented in this text clearly encourage us not to be anxious, to feel and share love, to be kind, to forgive those who hurt us most, and to nurture our spiritual being rather than our flesh. This is precisely what occurs when the reward system is stimulated, and even more interesting, it is these acts and behaviors that stimulate the reward system. Good begets good!

If the brain requires rhythm and balance to function at peak potential, it is critical to have the structures and processes in place to enable such balance. I find it interesting that the reward system is an older part of the brain, dating far back in our existence. What is new is our understanding of behavior and its relationship to the brain even though the prescription to internal balance and spiritual healing is thousands of years old. We do possess the structures, prescription, and ability to bring peace to our brains and bodies, which can be shared with others, and this is the underlying path for spiritual healing.

Neurospiritual Healing

I attended a Sunday mass at a local church in Aruba in late 2015. At the end of the mass, a female church leader rose and walked to the microphone, where she announced that her son who lives in the northeast of the United States was ill and that he was to undergo a fourth procedure Tuesday (December 8) for a brain tumor. She then asked everyone in the audience for their prayers. This struck me in a meaningful way as I supposed she could have asked for anything, or she could have simply remained quiet about her family's situation. That Tuesday, I kept her son in my prayers. Her request for prayer for her son indicates her faith that prayer can heal or at least bring comfort. Do you think any prescribing clinician has ever prescribed prayer? I am sure he or she is out there, and if you know one, make sure you seek their treatment.

This belief of so many in the power of faith and prayer is not new, and you know that. This has been part of the human DNA for thousands of years, and it began with the teachings of Christ as outlined in some of the selected scripture passages I provided in this book. You might be further interested to know that during my talks across the earth over the past twenty years, I have asked my audiences a question: How does a loved one get well when they are told they have a terminal condition? I ask this question after I tell everyone that the doctor in this hypothetical situation is correct with the diagnosis and prognosis, so "The doctor was wrong" is not a choice for an answer. While this information is anecdotal, the responses come from over twenty-five thousand people of all backgrounds, and the responses are the same:

- Love
- Faith
- Will to live
- Family
- Attitude
- God
- Prayer

Perhaps as striking is what people do not say. They do not say medication, inpatient hospitalization, chemotherapy, radiation, etc. The responses from my audience members have nothing to do with medicine, at least as we define *medical care* in the United States. The responses form the core virtues and values of what it means to be human and what is most important to us as humans. At this point, I make the statement to my audiences that these responses are heard all across the land and indicate a rather robust consensus on what the consumer indicates is needed for healing and health. Yet we do not integrate these medicines into our system of care.

Recall that the brain simply processes information; and something like love, the will to live, faith, and prayer affect the neurochemistry and behavior of the brain. As I stated earlier in this book, the message originating from the brain in the form of a thought represents the blueprint for action for the rest of the body. If the message is, "I have a will to live," then we should not be surprised when the body lives! It is true that this is not 100 percent guaranteed; however, it happens enough that most people around you have a story to share that will support my anecdotal finding.

All of this is presented to set the foundation for the power of neurospiritual healing and how our beliefs, thoughts, convictions, and behaviors affect particular regions of our brain to promote internal healing and outward sharing of the power of faith for others to also heal. In the context of this book, *healing* does not necessarily mean "cure of a human condition"; for I believe that the brain was granted by God and that his Son, Jesus, taught us that there is a distinct difference between the flesh and the Spirit. This section refers to neurospiritual healing that supersedes the flesh and the earth bound, recognizing that our salvation is spiritually based.

Having said that, I also believe that spirituality can heal conditions of the human body, and there are plenty of examples of this dating well before our time (see the scripture passages on faith above). Today we refer to these cases as *miracles* because we cannot explain how a cure or healing occurs when the textbooks or science say it is not possible. If science were to study miracles and integrate the power of spirituality, faith, and religion into medicine, they too would understand what a miracle is.

I have presented a case for neurospiritual healing, though I am not the author of this case. I am simply reminding all about the teachings of Jesus many years ago and how I believe there is a direct brain-behavior relationship. Our brain has critical regions known as the reward system (see fig. 3) that are located in the older parts of the brain. The reward system interacts with specific areas of the cortex (see fig. 4), and when triggered, the reward system provides euphoria, joy, love, balance, forgiveness, kindness, hope, and peace

Interestingly, the Fruits of the Spirit as outlined by St. Paul and described above represent the core of my *prescription for neurospiritual healing* because it is precisely the acts of love, forgiveness, faith, kindness, humility, and hope that trigger the reward system. There is a natural circle of specific behaviors (Fruits of the Spirit) and resulting euphoria and joy that represent spiritual healing and internal balance. This is what Jesus encouraged all to experience and to refrain from the anxieties of life. Anxieties come from an overactivation of the regions of the brain that promote comparative analysis of self and other, judgment, and moral review (see fig. 4). The teachings of Jesus do represent the path to neurospiritual healing, and our brain has the structures and neurochemical processes (reward system) to facilitate our journey on this path.

My prescription for neurospiritual healing is critical for all to follow and to integrate into their daily lives. There is indeed so much searching for answers, for quick fixes, for products and procedures to make us whole, to reduce our anxiety and sense of being incomplete. I see this in so many people, particularly the younger generation, which is upsetting. I want this book to be comforting to all who read it so each person knows all the answers to their questions and insecurities.

You have the hardware and software granted you by a Higher Being, and they sit in your brain and remain with you at all times. We have been taught how to behave and to feel, and we now know what happens in the brain when we act and feel a certain way. There is indeed a direct relationship between our behavior and brain functioning. I have proposed a prescription for neurospiritual healing that follows the Fruits of the Holy Spirit as a direct path for removing anxiety and insecurity, for becoming whole and integrated, and for feeling the euphoria, love, joy, and peace that Jesus wants us to feel.

My neurospiritual prescription requires that you engage in daily acts of *kindness* and *humility*; *forgive* all and particularly those who trespass against you; *love* and express love to all in your life; be *hopeful*, especially in difficult times, knowing that your behavior and faith will lead to your salvation; and always have *faith* in yourself and in the teachings of Jesus.

In living a life filled with the Fruits of the Holy Spirit, you will separate from self and all the earthbound bondage that selfishness can bring. My prescription for spiritual healing is anchored in acts for others and the positive and peaceful feelings that you will experience internally (reward system), which ultimately brings balance and homeostasis to your brain and body. Your neurospiritual health can then be shared with others who are in need, and this whole circle of healing becomes contagious as it always was meant to be.

I encourage all the healing professions to more formally integrate spiritual healing into your toolbox of care. The consumer is in need and is now desirous of more complete and holistic approaches to health and well-being. Have the courage to discuss openly the patient's spirituality, faith, and ability to follow the Fruits of the Holy Spirit. Prescribe the neurospiritual path as articulated in this book as a primary or ancillary treatment to all your patients, regardless of condition, age, or background. You will be helping your patient practice a life of joy, kindness, love, forgiveness, humility, and hope. There is no side effect; and with consistent firing of the reward system, the negativity of anxiety, insecurity, hopelessness, judgment, anger, bitterness, and evil will dissipate, leaving a more balanced brain and body.

A Final Thought

We are a beautiful species very capable of remarkable things, and yet we engage in behaviors that are destructive and hurtful. So many are filled with worry, fear, anxiety, and insecurity. Thousands are paying large sums of money for quick fixes that have very little, if any, evidence that they are helpful to our health. In all, there is a tidal wave of "searching" for something that will bring even a little relief. I fear we have lost the understanding that our power to be complete, secure, and balanced is within us and, more specifically, within our brain.

My career began in a very traditional manner, and I am blessed to have had the opportunity to study many years about human behavior and the human brain. I have been taught by the best and continue to be fueled by my colleagues and mentors. Over the past twenty years, I have been led to make two significant pivots away from my traditional career. First, I was led to speak, write, and think about the miracle that is the human brain and to educate the general public about this miracle that sits between our ears and how we can shape the brain for health all across the life span. This provided me opportunities to work with many sectors of society and to make small impacts on the lives of others that my traditional path never would have permitted. Now I am being led to make a second pivot that has me thinking, writing, and speaking about the purpose of my brain. This is a highly spiritual journey for me, and one that I feel so blessed to be a part of.

I hope my book provides deep thought and reflection on matters that go directly to our identity as humans and to our place in a grand universe and indeed to our salvation. I believe God granted us a brain for the grand purpose of communicating with him, healing within, and helping others heal. I further believe that Jesus taught us many years ago how we are to live our lives and that by living our lives based on his teachings, our reward system (see fig. 3) will provide us with peace, love, joy, and euphoria so necessary for spiritual health. In turn, by following the prescription for neurospiritual healing as outlined in this book, we have a specific blueprint to such healing and the potential to erode the anger, bitterness, hatred, and evil that is so present in our world today.

The ideas in this book are rather basic, yet they are profound in so many ways and deserve introspection, discussion, and even healthy debate. I believe our nation— and, indeed, the world—is in desperate need for love, forgiveness, kindness, humility, hope, and faith. Humans are humans, and this prescription is equally valid for anyone regardless of background or belief. I am hopeful that there is a strong yearning for this message and for an open discussion about what makes us human and what we so desperately need to unite as humans. Life is so short and precious and salvation so critical that a time-out on earth might be useful for all of us to talk about love, forgiveness, and hope as a starter.

My hope is derived from my direct and personal experiences with so many people on an international stage, and I believe the timing is ripe for this message and prescription. We must ignite our spiritual health and return to some basics that are truly the important elements of our identity. I ask that you love a little more, perform random acts of kindness, forgive those who have hurt you, remain humble, have faith in yourself and God, and never lose hope. We hold in our brains the answers to healing, world peace, and indeed, salvation. Begin today with love as it is the most powerful medicine of all!

Love one another as I have loved you.

—John 13:34

References

Anxiety and Depression Association of America. www.ADAA.org.

Black, K., and A. Mann. 2009. *Brain Surgeon*. New York: Wellness Central Publishing.

Brain Health Center. www.brainhealthctr.com.

Center for Disease Control. "Mental Health." www.CDC.gov.com.

Clark, B. C., N. K. Mahato, M. Nakazawa, T. D. Law, and J. S. Thomas. 2014. "The

Power of the Mind: The Cortex As a Critical Determinant of Muscle Strength/Weakness." *Journal of Neurophysiology* 112: 3219–3226.

Esch, T., and G. B. Stefano. 2005. "The Neurobiology of Love." *Neuroendocrinology Letters* 26:175–192.

Francesco, F., and A. Cervone. 2014. "Neurobiology of Love." *Psychiatria Danubina* 26: 266–268.

Graziano, M. S. 2010. God, Soul, Mind, Brain. Teaticket, MA: Leapfrog Press.

Greenberg, P. E., T. Sisitsky, R. C. Kessler, S. N. Finkelstein, E. R. Berndt, R. T. Davidson, J. C. Ballenger, and A. J. Fyer. 1999. "The Economic Burden of Anxiety Disorders in the 1990s." *Journal of Clinical Psychiatry* 60: 427–435.

Haggerty, B. B. 2009. *Fingerprints of God.* New York, NY: Penguin Books.

Hamilton, A. J. 2009. *The Scalpel and the Soul.* New York, NY: Penguin Books.

Hanson, R., and R. Mendius. 2009. *Buddha's Brain: The Practical Neuroscience of Happiness, Love, and Wisdom.* Oakland, Ca.: New Harbinger Publications.

Henson, B., H. Bernien, A. E. Dréau, A. Reiserer, N. Kalb, M. S. Blok, J. Ruitenberg, R. F. L. Vermeulen, R. N. Schouten, C. Abellán, W. Amaya, V. Pruneri, M. W. Mitchell, M. Markham, D. J. Twitchen, D. Elkouss, S. Wehner, T. H. Taminiau, and R. Hanson. 2015. "Experimental Loophole-free Violation of a Bell Inequality Using Entangled Electron Spins Separated by 1.3 Kilometres." *Nature* 526: 682–686.

Hill, R. M. 2009. *Neurotheology Revealst the Covert Bondage of Unforgiveness.* Lexington, KY: Rosie Hill.

Koenig, H. G. 1999. *The Healing Power of Faith.* New York, NY: Simon and Schuster.

Naskar, A. 2015. *The God Parasite.* United Kingdom: Amazon Publishing.

National Institute of Mental Health. www.nimh.nih.gov.

Newberg, A., and M. R. Waldman. 2010. *How God Changes Your Brain*. New York, NY: Ballantine Books.

Nussbaum, P. D. 2003. *Brain Health and Wellness*. Tarentum, PA: Word Association Press.

Nussbaum, P. D. 2010. *Save Your Brain*. New York: McGraw Hill.

Nussbaum, P. D. 2011. Neurosciences of the aging brain: Perspectives on brain health lifestyle. (Guest Editor). *Generations, 35, 2.*

Siegel, B. S. 2002. *Love, Medicine, and Miracles*. New York, NY: Quill Publishing.

The New American Bible (St. Joseph Edition) 1970. Catholic Book Publishing.

Visual Anatomy. www.visualanatomy.com.

Wilson, R. S. 2011. Mental Stimulation and Brain Health: Complex, Challenging Activities Can Support Cognitive Health in Older Adults. *Generations, 58-62.*

World Health Organization: www.who.int

Zeki, S. 2007. "The Neurobiology of Love." *Federation of European Biochemical Societies Letters* 581, 2575–2579.

Zohar, D. 1990. *The Quantum Self.* New York, NY: Quill Publishing.

APPENDIX 1

Recipes for a Healthy Brain and a Healthy You

As is the case with my recent books, I include a section on food! We all love to eat, and there is so much about food that is health related. It is also true that the Bible is filled with reference to food, the meal, and socialization. There is reference to the bread and wine as the body and blood of Christ and, of course, the Last Supper. I am most interested in foods for brain health, but food is also important for socialization, intimacy, recreation, and storytelling. Food can be novel and complex as we try different types of food, and we can get creative by trying to cook a meal or two ourselves!

I am pleased to have Rita Singer, RD, contribute some of her favorite recipes for your consideration and pleasure. Rita serves as the director of nutrition for my Brain Health Center (www.brainhealthctr.com), and she also has her own business, Red Dietitians (www.reddietitians.com).

Asian-Style Tuna Steaks

2 4-ounces tuna steaks
2 teaspoons Dijon mustard
1 teaspoon ground ginger
1 tablespoon liquid aminos or tamari
¼ cup fresh lemon juice
1 teaspoon sesame oil
¼ cup avocado oil
2 teaspoon sesame seeds

Combine mustard, ginger, liquid aminos, sesame oil, avocado oil, lemon juice, and sesame seeds in small mixing bowl. Place tuna steaks in small bowl. Add sauce to steaks and marinade 20 minutes. Prepare grill. Place steaks on grill and sear each side for 2–3 minutes for medium rare or longer for medium well.

Serves 2.

Calories: 270
Fat: 12 g
Carbohydrates: 2 g
Dietary Fiber: 0g

Protein: 35 g
Sodium: 480 mg

Avocado, Olive, and Tomato Salad

2 avocados, pits and peels removed and sliced
¼ cup large green pitted olives, no sugar added, sliced in half
¼ cup chopped red onion
¼ cup cherry tomatoes, halved
1 tablespoon fresh lemon juice
2 teaspoon white wine vinegar
1 teaspoon garlic powder
1 teaspoon fresh ground pepper
1 tablespoon chopped fresh parsley

Combine above ingredients in medium bowl. Serve chilled or
at room temperature.

Serves 4.

Calories: 150
Fat: 13 g
Saturated fat: 1.5 g
Carbohydrates: 10 g
Fiber: 6 g
Protein: 2 g
Sodium: 250 mg

Brain-Boosting Smoothie

1 cup fresh or frozen berries

6 ounces plain Greek yogurt

1 cup coconut water

2 teaspoon spirulina powder

1 banana

½ cup kale or spinach

Combine ingredients in a blender.
Serves 2.

Calories: 160

Fat: 1 g

Carbohydrates: 30 g

Sugar: 18 g

Dietary fiber: 5 g

Protein: 11 g

Sodium: 190 mg

Brussels Sprouts with Dijon Mustard and Toasted Pecans

1 pound brussels sprouts, washed and halved

1 tablespoon Dijon mustard

2 teaspoon olive oil, plus one tablespoon

2 teaspoon balsamic vinegar

1 clove garlic, minced
1 tablespoon fresh chopped dill
2 tablespoon chopped pecans

Heat 1 tablespoon olive oil over medium heat. Add brussels sprouts and cover for 5 minutes. In separate bowl, combine mustard, oil, and garlic. Add brussels sprouts and coat evenly. Add back to pan and continue to sauté for approximately 5 minutes or until lightly browned. Meanwhile, heat small sauté pan. Add pecans and dry roast for about 2 minutes until golden brown. Remove immediately. Add to brussels sprouts along with fresh dill and vinegar. Serve warm or at room temperature.

Serves 4.

Calories: 110
Fat: 5 g
Saturated fat: 0.5
Carbohydrates: 10 g
Fiber: 5 g
Protein: 3 g
Sodium: 125 mg

Bulgur Pilaf with Roasted Veggies

1 ¼ cups water
½ cup uncooked bulgur

2 sun-dried tomatoes, chopped
2 tablespoons pine nuts
1 tablespoon olive oil
1 medium onion, chopped
2 garlic cloves, coarsely chopped
½ teaspoon crushed red pepper
1 cup chopped zucchini
1 cup chopped eggplant
1 cup sliced mushrooms
½ cup chopped kalamata olives
2 tablespoon fresh parsley, chopped
salt
pepper

In a medium saucepan, bring water to a boil. Stir in bulgur. Reduce heat and simmer. Cover for 15 minutes or until water is absorbed.

Meanwhile, place zucchini, eggplant, mushrooms, garlic, onion, and olive oil on baking sheet. Place in oven and broil for 10 minutes.

In a small saucepan, dry roast pine nuts for 2 minutes, or until lightly browned, stirring constantly. Transfer to another plate and set aside.

Transfer bulgur to medium bowl and add sun-dried tomatoes, olives, pine nuts, and parsley. Mix in vegetables. Season to taste and serve.

Serves 4.

Cauliflower Leek and Potato Soup

4–5 medium Yukon Gold potatoes, peeled and cubed

½ cup chopped leeks

2 cups coarsely chopped cauliflower

1 garlic clove, chopped

4 fresh sage leaves, chopped

1 tablespoon fresh rosemary, chopped

1 tablespoon fresh thyme, chopped

½ cup cashew milk

4 cups low-sodium organic vegetable broth

2 teaspoon extravirgin olive oil

salt

pepper

Heat olive oil in a medium saucepan. Add potatoes, leeks, garlic, salt and pepper. Sauté for approximately 5–8 minutes over medium-high heat. Add broth and fresh herbs. Cook for 10 more minutes or until potatoes begin to soften. Add cauliflower and continue to cook until soft. Reduce heat to medium and add cashew milk and heat for another 2–3 minutes. Season to taste. Remove from heat, and in 2 small batches, add to blender and puree until smooth. Add back to pot and serve.

Optional extras:

    1 teaspoon crumbled blue cheese

1 teaspoon roasted nuts or seeds (pepitas, pine nuts, butternut
squash, pumpkin)
Fresh chopped sage

Calories: 130
Total fat: 2.5 g
Carbohydrates: 23 g
Dietary fiber: 3 g
Protein: 3 g
Sodium: 160 mg

Coconut Almond Granola

Dry ingredients:
¾ cup almond flour
¾ cup coconut flour
4 cups slivered almonds
1 cup pepitas
½ cup sunflower seeds
1 cup walnuts
3 cups shredded unsweetened coconut
2 teaspoon cinnamon
1 teaspoon ground ginger
1 teaspoon sea salt (optional)

Wet ingredients:
1 cup unrefined organic coconut oil, heated

½ honey or maple syrup
3 teaspoon pure vanilla extract

Preheat oven to 250 degrees Fahrenheit.

Combine dry ingredients in large bowl and mix. Whisk together wet ingredients and add to dry ingredients, mixing to coat.

Spread granola on two individual baking sheets. Place in oven for 60 minutes. Remove and enjoy as a snack, on yogurt or with milk.

(You can use all-almond flour or all-coconut flour.)

Serves approximately 50 (¼ cup per serving).

Calories: 170
Total fat: 15 g
Carbohydrates: 7 g
Dietary fiber: 2 g
Protein: 4 g
Sodium: 40 mg

Couscous and Lentil Salad

1 cup green lentils
1 cup whole wheat couscous, dry
½ cup fresh lemon juice
3 tablespoons balsamic vinegar
2 tablespoon spoon extravirgin olive oil

2 garlic cloves, minced
4 scallions, white and green parts, chopped
1 pint cherry tomatoes, sliced in half
2 tablespoon fresh basil
1 tablespoon fresh parsley
sea salt (optional)
½ avocado, sliced
2 cups fresh arugula
1tablespoon feta (optional)

Combine lentils with 2 ½ cups water and bring to a boil. Cover slightly and simmer for 20–25 minutes until soft. Run under cold water and drain. Meanwhile, in a small saucepan, boil 1 cup water. When water boils, add couscous, remove from heat, and cover for 5 minutes. Mix lentils and couscous. Allow to cool. Whisk lemon juice, vinegar, oil, and garlic in small bowl. Pour over lentils and couscous and mix well. Add scallions, cherry tomatoes, basil, and parsley. Season with salt. Mix in arugula, avocado, and feta cheese. Serve.

Serves 6 (1 cup per serving).

Calories: 260
Total fat: 8 g
Protein: 11 g
Carbohydrates: 39 g
Fiber: 9 g
Sodium: 30 mg

Roasted Beet and Mint Salad with Goat Cheese and Pistachios

1 bunch beets
2 cup arugula, washed and dried
1 tablespoon fresh mint, chopped
1 ounce goat cheese crumbles
¼ cup pistachios, chopped
2 teaspoon fig balsamic vinegar

Preheat oven to 375 degrees Fahrenheit. Wash beets and remove stems by cutting the top of the beet along with the greens. (Don't throw them away! Beet greens are great sautéed with olive oil and garlic!) Fill an 8×8 baking dish with 1–2 in water and place beets stem side down (the part you removed). Roast for 1 hour.

Remove from the oven and, using your hands, peel off the skins (you will know the beets are ready when the skin is easily removed). Slice in 1-inch circles.

Arrange arugula on a plate, add beets, and top with fresh mint, goat cheese, and balsamic vinegar.

Buen provecho!
4 Servings

Calories: 120
Total fat: 7 g
Carbohydrates: 11 g

Dietary fiber: 3 g
Protein: 5 g
Sodium: 170 mg

Fresh Mediterranean Salad
with Grilled Octopus

1 pound octopus
2 baby red potatoes, diced
¼ cup fennel, chopped
¼ cup red pepper, diced
1 tablespoon fresh parsley, chopped
1 celery stalk, chopped
¼ cup kalamata olives, sliced in half
2 tablespoon capers
1 tablespoon red onion, chopped
1 cup arugula
½ freshly squeezed lemon
1 teaspoon red wine vinegar
2 tablespoon olive oil
salt
pepper

Preheat grill. Brush octopus with olive oil and season with dash of salt and pepper. In medium sauté pan, heat 1 tablespoon olive oil. Add potatoes and season with salt and pepper. Cover and cook for about 10 minutes or until soft.

Meanwhile, combine fennel, pepper, parsley, celery, olives capers, olive oil, and onion in bowl. Add to potatoes and mix together for about 2 minutes. Remove from heat. Add arugula, lemon juice, and red wine vinegar. Season to taste.

Place octopus on hot grill and grill quickly until it browns on the outside. Remove and slice. Add to salad and serve.

6 Servings

Calories: 150
Total fat: 7 g
Carbohydrates: 9 g
Dietary fiber: 1 g
Protein: 12 g
Sodium: 350 mg

Leg of Lamb with Rosemary and Garlic

1 3-pound boneless organic grass-fed leg of lamb
2 tablespoon fresh rosemary
1 tablespoon Dijon mustard
5 cloves garlic, minced
1 tablespoon organic grass-fed butter or extravirgin olive oil
2 teaspoon freshly ground pepper
1 teaspoon sea salt

In a food processor or blender, combine rosemary, mustard, garlic, olive oil or butter, pepper and salt. Apply to lamb, cover and marinate 30 minutes at room temperature.

Preheat oven to 450 degrees Fahrenheit. Put lamb in oven safe dish and place in oven on the middle rack. Roast lamb for about 1 hour or until center of meat registers 145 degrees Fahrenheit for medium rare. Remove from oven and let sit for 10 minutes before carving.

Serves 6–8.

Calories: 230
Fat: 8 g
Saturated fat: 3 g
Carbohydrates: 1 g
Dietary fiber: 0 g
Protein: 36 g
Sodium: 360 mg

Lentil Soup

1 cup dry lentils, rinsed and drained
1 cup green bell pepper, chopped
2 medium carrots, chopped
1 medium onion, chopped
½ teaspoon dried sage, crushed
¼ teaspoon ground red pepper
3 garlic cloves, minced
2 ½ cups organic low-sodium chicken broth
2 ½ cups water

In large pot, mix lentils, sweet pepper, carrots, onion, sage, ground red pepper, garlic, chicken broth, and water. Bring to a boil, reduce heat. Cover and simmer for 20–25 minutes or until vegetables and lentils are tender.

Serves 5 (1 ¼ cup per serving).

Calories: 150
Fat: 1 g
Carbohydrates: 29 g
Dietary Fiber: 7 g
Protein: 9 g
Sodium: 250 mg

Orange-Ginger Halibut

1 pound halibut
2 cups orange juice
2 teaspoon freshly grated ginger
1 teaspoon grated lime zest
2 garlic cloves, chopped
Preheat oven to 450 degrees Fahrenheit.

Combine orange juice, ginger, lime rind, and garlic in medium bowl. Add fillet and marinade in refrigerator for 20–30 minutes. Place entire halibut and marinade in small baking dish and cook for 12–14 minutes or until fish flakes easily when tested with a fork.

Serves 4.

Calories: 180
Fat: 2.5 g
Carbohydrates: 14 g
Dietary fiber: 0 g
Protein: 24 g
Sodium: 75 mg

Quinoa with Apples and Cinnamon

1 cup quinoa
1 cup chopped apples with skin
½ teaspoon cinnamon
2 teaspoon 100% maple syrup
½ cup ground walnuts

Combine quinoa with 2 cups water. Add remaining ingredients. Bring to a boil. Cover and simmer for 12–15 minutes until quinoa is cooked. Serve.

Serves 4.

Calories: 170
Fat: 5 g
Carbohydrates: 26 g
Fiber: 4 g
Protein: 5 g
Sodium: 5 mg

Walnut-Encrusted Salmon

4 4-ouncde salmon fillets
¼ cup walnuts
1 tablespoon apple butter
1 tablespoon Dijon mustard
¼ teaspoon coarse black pepper
1 tablespoon fresh thyme

Preheat oven to 450 degrees Fahrenheit. Place walnuts on baking sheet and toast for 5 minutes until lightly browned. Remove immediately and place in food processer to finely chop walnuts. Combine apple butter, mustard, pepper, and thyme in small bowl. Place salmon filets on baking dish and brush with apple-butter mixture. Top with toasted walnuts and bake 14–15 minutes or until salmon flakes.

Serves 4.

Calories: 220
Fat: 12g
Carbohydrates: 4 g
Dietary fiber: 1 g
Protein: 24 g
Sodium: 140 mg

Savory Bean Soup

1 teaspoon olive oil

½ cup red onion, chopped

2 celery stocks, chopped

2 carrots, chopped

2 garlic cloves, chopped

1 cup organic low-sodium chicken broth

2 cups water

1 15-ounce can chickpeas or navy beans, rinsed and drained

1 14.5-ounce can no-salt-added diced tomatoes, drained

¼ teaspoon crushed red pepper flakes (optional)

1 teaspoon dried oregano

1 teaspoon dried thyme

2 cups fresh spinach or kale

¼ cup freshly grated parmesan or Romano cheese

In a large saucepan, heat olive oil over medium heat. Add onion, celery, and garlic for 5–6 minutes or until onion and celery are tender and garlic is golden brown. Stir in broth, water, beans, tomatoes, oregano, thyme, and red pepper flakes. Bring to a boil then reduce heat and simmer for 20–25 minutes. Stir in spinach or kale and simmer, covered for until wilted. Serve with parmesan cheese.

Serves 6 (1 cup per serving).

Calories: 150
Fat: 2.5 g
Carbohydrates: 20 g
Fiber: 4 g
Protein: 8 g
Sodium: 240 mg

Spaghetti Squash with Roasted Veggies and Parmesan

1 spaghetti squash, halved and seeded
1 tablespoon extravirgin olive oil
2 tablespoon fresh lemon juice
1 shallot, chopped
2 garlic cloves, chopped
¼ teaspoon crushed red pepper (optional)
1 ½ cup chopped fresh tomatoes or 15-ounce can diced
    tomatoes, drained
2 tablespoon fresh basil
1 yellow pepper, chopped
1 cup chopped asparagus
1 cup sliced mushrooms
¼ teaspoon ground fresh pepper
2 tablespoon sliced black olives
1 tablespoon grated parmesan cheese

Preheat oven to 375 degrees Fahrenheit. Place spaghetti squash facedown on baking sheet and place in oven for about 30 minutes or until soft. Remove squash and set aside to cool. Turn oven to broil.

In small bowl, mix yellow pepper, mushrooms, and asparagus with 2 teaspoon olive oil and fresh ground pepper. Pour veggies onto baking sheet and place in oven for 10 minutes.

Meanwhile, heat 1 teaspoon oil in medium skillet. Add shallot, garlic, and red pepper. Sauté for 2 minutes. Add tomatoes and basil and cook for about 3 minutes. Remove veggies from oven. Use a fork to scoop out the stringy pulp from the squash and place in medium bowl. Add veggies and tomato mixture. Top with black olives and parmesan cheese and mix. Serve hot.

Serves 4.

Calories: 110
Fat: 3.5 g
Saturated fat: 1 g
Carbohydrates: 17 g
Dietary fiber: 3 g
Protein: 4 g
Sodium: 230 mg

Spinach with Chickpeas
Espinacas con Garbanzos
(A Spanish Favorite)

2 pounds fresh spinach

15-ounce chickpeas (garbanzo beans), rinsed and drained

1 tablespoon olive oil, plus 2 teaspoons

2 cloves garlic, minced

2 teaspoons cumin

1 slice whole grain bread or gluten-free bread, optional (best if 1–2 days old)

2 teaspoons paprika

Steam spinach. Remove from heat and pour out most of the water, but not all of it, about 1 tablespoon. Place spinach in medium pot with chickpeas. Set aside.

Next, in a small skillet, add 1 tablespoon olive oil and heat. Add garlic cloves and sauté until light brown, about 1–2 minutes. Remove garlic from pan using spoon and place in a small bowl or mortar. Now add bread slice to same skillet used to brown garlic until crispy and toasted. Place in bowl with garlic. Add to bowl cumin and liquid from the spinach. Mash until a paste is formed (does not have to be completely mashed to bits). Add to spinach and chickpeas.

Now add 2 teaspoons olive oil to small skillet again and heat. Add paprika and whoosh around in skillet for 5–10 seconds until it becomes a darker red. Remove immediately and add to spinach pot. Mix whole spinach mixture and turn on heat. Simmer 5–10 minutes.

Serves 4 (1 cup per serving).

Calories: 180
Fat: 7 g
Carbohydrates: 24 g
Dietary fiber: 5 g
Protein: 7 g
Sodium: 85 mg

Vegetarian Chili

1 tablespoon avocado oil
2 cloves garlic, minced
1 cup red onion, chopped
1 green bell pepper, chopped
1 tablespoon chili powder
1 tablespoon cumin
1 28-ouce can no-salt-added chopped tomatoes
1 15-ounce can kidney beans, washed and drained
1 15-oz can black beans, washed and drained
1-15 ounce can garbanzo beans, washed and drained
1 teaspoon red pepper flakes (optional)
½ cup fresh or frozen corn
½ teaspoon chia seeds

Combine oil, garlic, onion, and peppers in a medium pot over heat. Add red pepper flakes and chili powder, mixing well. Add tomatoes, beans, and corn. Bring to a boil. Add chia seeds. Simmer for at least 20–30 minutes. Serve.

Serves 8 (1 cup per serving).

Calories: 210
Fat: 2.5 g
Carbohydrates: 37 g
Dietary fiber: 11 g
Protein: 11 g
Sodium: 40 mg

Spring Veggie Stir-Fry

5-ounce extrafirm tofu, cubed
½ cup orange juice
1 tablespoon liquid aminos
1tablespoon freshly grated ginger or 2 teaspoon ground ginger
2 cloves garlic, minced
1 tablespoon sesame seeds
2 tablespoon sesame oil
1 medium red pepper, sliced
1 cup edamame
½ medium yellow onion, sliced
8 ounces cremini mushrooms, sliced
2 cups cooked quinoa

Combine tofu, orange juice, liquid aminos, ginger, garlic, and sesame seeds in a medium bowl and marinate in refrigerator for 30 minutes. Heat a wok or a skillet to medium high. Add sesame oil, pepper, mushrooms, edamame, and onion. Cook until tender but crisp. Add tofu and marinade. Cook for 5–7 minutes or until tofu is cooked. Serve over quinoa.

Serves 4.

Calories 320
Total Fat 13g
Sat Fat 1.5g
Total Carb 35g
Dietary Fiber 5g
Protein 15g
Sodium 220mg

APPENDIX 2

Nature's Gifts and Our Neurospiritual Healing

Spiritual healing as experienced in my travels over the years.

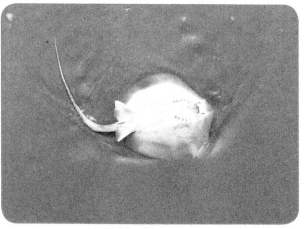

Our Lady of Alta Vista in Aruba

About the Author

Dr. Nussbaum is a clinical neuropsychologist. He is an Adjunct Professor of Neurological Surgery at the University of Pittsburgh School of Medicine. Dr. Nussbaum has spent the past fifteen years educating the general public about the miracle of the human brain and how to shape it for health across the entire lifespan (www.brainhealthctr.com).

Dr. Nussbaum's work provides ideas on the important role the human brain may play in our spiritual health and in our ability to both feel and share the greatest medicines of all: love, forgiveness, kindness, faith, humility, and hope. His call is to bring the teachings of Jesus to everyone regardless of background, to raise a call to action to all clinicians, and to explain a most grand purpose for our having a brain.

CPSIA information can be obtained at www.ICGtesting.com
Printed in the USA
BVOW06s0023080716

454465BV00003B/3/P